My Perfect Broken God

My Perfect Broken God

Musings of a Former Believer

Brent MacLean

RJ West Publishing
2019

First Printing: 2019

ISBN: 978-0-359-66471-9

RJ West Publishing

For Jessica

Never stop asking questions

Dear God if someone is trying to hurt me could you protect me. I'll do anything you want! if I do somthing wrong would you forgive me. I love you. So I'll do the Ten Commandments. I'll do anything. Just help me.

Written by the author at age 7

Acknowledgements

This book developed from a blog I operated over a 4 year period and I'd be remiss if I didn't express my gratitude to the readers. Whether you were a constant reader of <u>My Perfect Broken Mind</u> or someone that read a single post, I would like to say thank you. This book would not exist without your interest and support.

I would like to thank Mark Hoyles, both for the encouragement and for reading through a near-final draft, helping to set my mind at ease that this stuff made sense and my message was clear.

I also want to thank Roz French. You were always interested in whatever I had to say, even if you disagreed (which didn't seem to be very often). It was reassuring to know someone who was totally open to any new idea I might be rambling about, no matter how wacky or outside the norm. Thank you. It meant more to me than you realized.

I'd like to acknowledge the support of my wife, Alison. It would be impossible to express in a few sentences how grateful I am for your love and patience throughout the past twenty years. Thank you and I love you.

Finally, I want to thank my daughter, Jessica. Your inquisitive nature and desire to learn as much as you can about the world is a constant inspiration. I hope that years down the road you feel pride when you realize that without even knowing it you helped Daddy write his very first book. I love you more than I could ever say.

Preface

I started <u>My Perfect Broken Mind</u> in February 2011. I wasn't a fan of personal blogs, my experience with them relegated to "Mommy Blogs", the sort that do nothing more than extol the virtues of breeding. But I figured I'd give it a go anyway and began copying and pasting about 230 pieces that I had already written. Then I just kept writing whenever the mood hit me. Turns out the mood hit me a lot, because the blog soon amassed over 1500 posts. There wasn't much I wouldn't write about. The original Google search description read "a blog about language & communication, religion & atheism, trends & traditions, art & music, political correctness & truth, social norms & social networks, love & relationships, intelligence & stupidity". The topic I tackled most was language and communication. I've always had an interest in language. Words, sayings, accents, dialects, slang, and euphemisms are fascinating to me, and I loved pointing out the interesting—and often silly—aspects of each; things the average person never stopped to ponder. But, perhaps not surprisingly, the posts about religion seemed to garner the most reaction from readers.

When I first attempted to compile posts for a book the idea was to have a wide range of topics, just as the blog was. This turned out to be far too monumental a task. The first "draft" of that book idea had well over 220,000 words. (The book you now hold in your hands is under 50,000 words in length.) So I knew I had to start whittling it down. I thought the best way to do this would be to focus on one topic, and what better topic than the one that people reacted to the most.

What may be most interesting about my lifelong interest in religion is how fervently I believed in it, despite coming from a family that wasn't really religious. My family was what some might call "culturally Christian". I usually refer to such folks as "religious moderates", which simply means they believe in God, but don't pay much attention to the particulars of whatever faith or denomination they happen to be connected to. My family, like every other family around us, celebrated Christmas, had weddings in churches, had their kids Christened, etc., but did little beyond that. We had Bibles in the house but no one ever read them (save for my brother's giant illustrated Children's Bible that I became quite obsessed with). We said our morning prayers in school, learned about baby Jesus at Christmas, and went on school trips to church on Easter. In fact, the only times I saw the inside of any churches outside these annual school trips were the one funeral I attended at the age of 5, and one very traumatic experience in a Pentecostal Tabernacle. (I consider it detrimental to a child's well-being to take them to church. I consider it *child abuse* to take them to a Pentecostal church.)

Perhaps the greatest source of my religious knowledge was my brother. Many a night he would dispense tidbits of his own Biblical insight, limited as it was. One of the most vivid of such memories is when he first explained the 10 Commandments to me. I was amazed. Rules blatantly listed designed to get me into heaven?! It fascinated me. But it also terrified me. I knew, try as I might, that I couldn't live up to God's standards, not 100%. Then there was the time my brother recited some spooky-sounding chant in an effort to coax the devil to show up in my bedroom that night. I only remember the last line: "... appear beside my bed tonight." It scared me, but I don't blame him one iota for the fear I felt as a child. Not at all. He was an older brother doing what older brothers do. He had no idea how gullible I was, or how much it would affect me. Besides, my mental state and well-being wasn't his concern. But I must admit I'm not quite as forgiving when it comes to adults. I think they could have made it clear to me that it was all nonsense. It wouldn't have taken long and it would have saved me a great deal of torment. As I said, I believed in it all, and I believed in it all because I trusted grownups. I was certain they wouldn't lie to a child about important things like God, heaven and my eternal soul. I believed it and I wanted it to be true. I wanted to *make sure* it was true. So as I got older I began looking into it, to solidify my beliefs, if nothing else. Slowly but surely I moved through stages of curiosity, suspicion, confusion, surprise, anger, and eventually relief. But a little bit of the anger remained. And that led to much of the writing contained in this book.

      Most of the posts in this book were written spontaneously, when something came across my radar that caused me to react in a certain way. That's how I preferred to write. It kept everything fresh and it was the easiest way to go about it. Once I get on a roll the words usually flow fast and free. So this book is definitely not a streamlined train of thought. I've aligned the posts in alphabetical order, save for the last two, which just so happen to be the last two posts I've ever written for My Perfect Broken Mind. There was no plan to stop blogging and I had no idea as I was writing them that they would be the final posts. But once they were done it all seemed... done. I felt that anything else I might write would simply be repeating myself. Initially I was a little despondent that the site I had worked on for almost 5 years was no more. But then I realized its absence freed me up to complete this book, as writing it was a constant series of ebbs and flows, starts and stops. But with the encouragement of a few friends and family, I was able to work my way through to see it finished. And I hope you enjoy it.

Brent MacLean
Corner Brook, Newfoundland
May 14, 2019

A Position on Faith –
Not a Position of Faith

If you've ever said, "Atheism is just another religion" it means you don't understand a very simple concept.

The word atheist comes from the term a-theist, meaning "not a theist". It's the same as amoral, which means "without morals". Atheism simply means one does not—the reasons are irrelevant—believe in any particular god or gods. That's it. There are no guidelines to follow, no buildings in which to gather once a week, no special book containing rules on what you can and cannot do, and no one or nothing to worship. It is not a religion.

Would you say the same thing about people that do not believe in aliens? What about the people that don't believe in unicorns? How about Bigfoot? I'm sure you wouldn't say "Ah, those Bigfoot-deniers got their own religion." See, the whole "I believe in God vs. I want evidence first" debate is not equally-sided. One side is making unrealistic and unfounded claims based on little or no evidence, while the other side is simply saying, "Give me a reason to believe and I will. If you don't have evidence then don't expect me to blindly believe what you say." Here's a definition of the word religion:

religion:

1. a set of beliefs concerning the cause, nature, and purpose of the universe, esp. when considered as the creation of a superhuman agent or agencies, usually involving devotional and ritual observances, and often containing a moral code governing the conduct of human affairs

2. a specific fundamental set of beliefs and practices generally agreed upon by a number of persons or sects

3. the body of persons adhering to a particular set of beliefs and practices.

See? I'm not adhering to any set of beliefs, I'm not adhering to any set of practices, I'm not concerning myself with anything "superhuman", I have no rituals, and my moral code is not derived from any book or other atheists.

I have no religion.

Answering is Impossible with Jesus

I posted the quote "No amount of belief makes something a fact" on the blog's Facebook page. In response a Christian lady wrote "Anything is possible with Jesus." Of course, I couldn't let that go unchallenged, what with it being my page and all. So challenge it I did.

What I want you to notice about her answer is how she answers without answering. Christians, and any religious people, really, often answer questions without actually answering them. If you ever get into a conversation with the Mormons that knock on your door you'll quickly encounter their circular reasoning. It can quickly become irritating, and eventually nauseating. It really is this old cliché:

> "God exists."
> "How do you know?"
> "Because it says so in the Bible."
> "How do you know the Bible is the truth?"
> "Because it's the Word of God."
> "Well, how do you know God is real?"
> "It says so in the Bible."
> "How do you know the Bible tells the truth?"
> "Because it's the Word of God."
> "But how do you know God exists?"

And on and on it goes. It's a cliché and a fallacy but it's utilized by millions of people. This *answering without answering* really fascinates me. I often wonder if deep down these people know the difference and it's actually a conscious avoidance of the question, whatever that question might be. Anyway, here is that lady's statement, my question, and her excellent response. (I'll leave out the rest of the conversation because it really wasn't one. I asked another question and she sent me lots of copy-and-paste jobs explaining how "we know biblical miracles really happened".)

> "Anything is possible with Jesus."
> "Can an amputee's arm grow back?"
> "With Jesus you can live happily without the arm."

Isn't that awesome?! Seriously, I love it. It's such a great example of answer avoidance. This lady, unless she's crazy, which I don't think she is, knows the answer is no. But she just *can't* concede. She cannot admit that "anything" is not possible, with or without Jesus. It's too bad this type of "logic" didn't work in school.

<u>Are You a Pedophile?</u>

I've had more than a few people imply that if you are an outspoken atheist it means you are secretly a believer, and that you are simply trying to convince yourself that there is no God.

Take a moment to read that again, if you like.

Seriously folks, where is the logic here? One woman said to me, "For an atheist you sure do talk about God a lot. Maybe you're trying to convince yourself there's no God?" Another person said, "It seems to me since you talk about God so much you're actually trying to convince yourself of what you say. If you believed what you said you wouldn't have to say it."

I must admit I sat confused for a few minutes after reading that last message. *If you believed what you said you wouldn't have to say it.* I mean, try applying that logic to another interest or cause that a person might be invested in. Take cancer, for instance. Would anyone ever say to a person that partakes in fundraising for cancer awareness, "Hey, for someone that says they're against cancer you sure do talk about it a lot. Maybe you actually like cancer and you're just trying to convince yourself you hate it, hmm?" Does that make any sense? What about people that are gung-ho for protecting children from molesters and pedophiles? Using that reasoning I could say, "Hey, Trudy. I gotta say.... you talk an awful lot about protecting kids from pedophiles.... I can't help but wonder..... are...... are *you* a pedophile?"

Brent MacLean

<u>Beliefs and the Button</u>

I love how people try to be all proper and politically correct by saying they don't care about a political candidate's religious beliefs. Well, you should care.

Say one of their beliefs is that "all infidels should be put to death". Call me nutty, but I would say people probably should care about that. It seems important. Especially for a politician with any sort of military might. If a candidate gets messages directly from God (like they all claim they do) and God tells them that "Jewish people are the enemies of the Almighty", then yeah, again, that seems like something the public should be concerned about.

<u>Believe it—Just Don't Say it's True</u>

These are some things I'm sure I'll be repeating for the rest of my life:

I don't care if someone believes in God. I don't care if they are religious. I don't care if they go to church.

I do care if they try to tell me that what they believe is true. Then I want them to present some proof or evidence.

I do care when adults force these unfounded beliefs on the fragile minds of children, which is still quite acceptable, even in our so-called "atheist country". I do care when people are cutting pieces off newborn children as some sort of covenant with God, under the guise of hygiene.

I do care when people insist on integrating religious beliefs into schools. I do care when laws and societal norms stem from outdated, fictional Bible stories and are used to oppress certain factions of the population, i.e. homosexuals, women, etc. That's when someone's belief gets in the way—when they claim something is true but will not or cannot present reason, and still expect the world around them to bend and change in accordance to the sexist, racist, immoral rules of their particular belief system.

<u>**Clones in the Garden of Eden**</u>

Just read a book written by a Christian ministry. The authors confidently claimed to know why atheists do not believe in God. They understand it completely they said. They also claimed that their intention was to show us why they believe as they do. It seemed like it might be interesting. Informative even. After the first two pages I thought, "Hmm. May be a sensible book."

Holy hell, it was INSANE! First they talk about the creation of the earth. God created it in "5 God days", it says. Then he created "a species called angels" and he hung around on earth with these angels for many earth years. These weren't the ol' people-with-wings angels like we're used to. These were the "real" ones. They were just like us. They even had the same type DNA we have. Long story short, one angel starts to get too confident. He rebels and starts a war between himself and God. Next God makes Adam and secludes him in a safe place. Well, Adam quickly gets bored so God becomes the first to experiment with cloning. (Yes, this is all in the book. I know it sounds like I'm embellishing for humor. I'm not.) But he changes the DNA profile just enough to make the person come out female. It's Eve. The spirits of God's enemies, Satan and his crew, begin stirring. Satan tempts Eve, Eve eats stuff she's not supposed to, and God loses his mind in anger. He "shook the earth" so much that he created mountain ranges and triggered an Ice Age.

And on and on their version goes. They go through some major points in the Bible, sprinkled with their own flair. They go through the 20th century as well and insert made-up reasons for why this or that happened, which basically equals out to *God did the good stuff, Satan did the bad.* Keep in mind that not one iota of evidence is presented for any of this. None.

They say at the beginning of the book that they know why atheists are atheists, but it quickly becomes clear they haven't much of a clue about atheists at all. So what makes them so eager to claim that they understand why so many people don't believe what they do? (It should be noted that they're not addressing only atheists, but everyone in the world that does not follow Jesus and the Bible; all other religions are lumped in with the atheists.) Well, according to them, the reason so many of us does not believe the same things they believe is quite simple: We've been tricked by Satan! Yup, that's it. It's the ol' Devil and his bag of tricks again. That's the big conclusion in this book. I and every other non-Christian in the world have been deceived. I actually had a pastor tell me this very thing a couple years ago—that Satan was working through me. I guess he was right.

I try to remain as objective as possible. I really do. I've read many parts of the Bible and am currently going through the whole thing (a task which is on hold until this book gets done). That's why I read these anti-atheism, pro-God books—just to get both sides. But all it has done is reinforced by disbelief. The more I research and question, the more I look at both sides, the more confident I become that religious people have nothing to hang their beliefs on. It's all made up. It's all nonsense. If anyone says they "know" God or what happens after we die they are completely full of shit. No one knows anything.

But then again, that might be just what the devil *wants* me to believe.

Close-Minded Free Thinkers

I recently saw a man's Facebook page on which he described himself as a "Freethinker". In his About Me section he had written "I think what I think and there isn't anyone in the world that can change that." Isn't that the most close-minded thing you've ever heard? He is the *opposite* of a freethinker. Is there anyone that can change *my* mind? Yes! Of course! Anyone can! In fact, I love having my mind changed by new ideas and opinions. Jesus, if I knew that everything I thought right now and every opinion I currently have was never going to change no matter what, heavens to Betsy, that would be atrocious. I wouldn't want to live the rest of my life knowing that my mind was so stagnant and unchanging.

In a similar vein, I saw a girl's profile that said her religious views were "Atheist – There is no God and you cannot convince me otherwise." Again, very narrow-minded. I don't feel this way at all. I'm an atheist, sure, but if someone or something demonstrates that there is a God or gods, then of course I'm going to change my opinion. Do I think there's a great chance of that actually happening? No, I do not. Do I believe my cat can sing Milli Vanilli songs? No, I do not. But if he suddenly gets up and belts out "Blame it on the rain, yeah, yeah", well, then I will instantly change my mind. Do I think that's likely to happen? Again, no, I don't. But that doesn't change the fact that given good and valid evidence, I will believe something is true.

Without reason to believe how can I possibly say it is so? By the same token, how can I expect to learn anything at all if my mind is completely closed to new ideas?

The Cosmic Fence-Sitters

Agnostics—here's my problem with them.

They often talk about how no one knows "100%" whether or not there is a God. But that should be a given. I could say that no one knows "100%" that there are no unicorns, because you cannot prove a negative. (I've heard it said that the only thing that can ever be 100% certain is math.) So are these people agnostic when it comes to unicorns? Would they correct you if you assumed that they didn't believe in unicorns? Would they say, "Now wait a minute. I didn't say I didn't believe in unicorns. Nobody knows *for sure* whether or not they exist."? Of course not. They don't believe in unicorns because there's no *reason* to believe in unicorns. And just because no one can offer any proof that unicorns do *not* exist, they don't say that when it comes to magical horses with horns "no one knows for sure". Would these people use this same logic when considering the existence of leprechauns? Dragons? Flying cats? Only with God do they suspend the reasoning we use where until there is a reason to believe positive, we will not live our lives as if the positive has been validated. People say, "You cannot prove there isn't a God." But the same can be said for anything that doesn't exist!

So when people say to me that there *could* be a God I say, "*Of course there could!*" But should I assume there *is* one just on that fact? Would I do that with any of the other non-existent creatures I mentioned above? No. With unicorns and the like we say, hey, there's no reason to think they exist so until it's proven that they do, I'm going to assume they don't. Only with God is it considered normal to reverse the logic.

Brent MacLean

<u>Crashing into Paradise</u>

I was stopped at a red light when I noticed the minivan ahead of me had a bumper sticker that read: *In Case of Rapture This Vehicle Will Be Unmanned.* This is the owner's cute way of telling everyone behind him that he's a Christian who's been *saved.* This simply means that God has chosen him specifically as one of the lucky few who will be granted entry into heaven once the world ends. The silly slogan is meant to imply that should the Rapture occur while the driver is in his van, he will disappear, leaving it driver-less. Besides the ridiculous notion of being saved—which is essentially just people *deciding* that they're good enough for God, and claiming to have his stamp of approval without a shred of evidence that he's actually cool with it—I think this driver is a complete asshole, and not just because the bumper sticker is actually his way of letting you know he's better than you. Really, "God chose me"? You cannot get more arrogant than that. No, I'm saying he's an asshole because by driving his car when he's so spectacularly saved he's endangering the lives of countless innocent people.

Okay, *I* don't think he's endangering lives, of course. But according to *his* claim of being saved, and the subsequent possibility of his disappearing while driving his vehicle, thus leaving it unattended, possibly while in motion, I think he's being a real prick for putting other drivers, those not lucky enough to be so loved by God, in such danger. Only a self-absorbed, pompous jerk would be so blatantly inconsiderate. Surely, God wouldn't favour such a selfish bastard. Right?

<u>Deadbook</u>

I can't be the only one weirded out when people use Facebook to communicate with the dead. Do they really think that dead people are checking Facebook? And is that what we have to look forward to after we die? More freakin' Facebook?

<u>Dear God,</u>
<u>Please Solidify Carol's Nose Mucus</u>

I just saw someone online asking for others to "send strong thoughts" to someone else that is sick. That might be even dumber than "sending positive vibes". Strong thoughts? What the hell are strong thoughts? And how are my thoughts, even if they're super-duper strong, supposed to help someone get healthier?

It reminds me of when I was a kid, this one boy I knew used to pretend he had healing powers. We went along with him, just because it was fun. But we were 7 years old! We all had super powers! And even then we really knew better. Now it boggles my mind. There's no way—*no way*—that sensible adults think that sending "strong thoughts" is going to rid someone else of their cancer or their ALS or their sore throat.

But that's another thing. If you believe sending strong thoughts or positive vibes or healing intentions actually helps rid others of serious diseases, why don't I ever see people doing it for common, more easily curable illnesses? No one's heart goes out to anyone with a headache. No one prays for someone's stuffy nose to unstuff. No one sends positive vibes to anyone to help heal their restless leg syndrome. It would seem that if you can help cure cancer with your mind, you would clear up everyday sicknesses in a snap.

Of course that inevitably leads to something I always wonder: why nobody prays for things we know are impossible. Have you ever noticed that? Ever think about that? People only pray for things that can actually clear up on their own, or with the help of medical science. Isn't that a coincidence? No one prays for Walter's amputated leg to grow back. Why not? God can't do such a thing? Your super awesome thoughts are strong enough to travel through space and kill someone's cancer cells but they can't regenerate cells to grow back missing limbs? Why is it that your magical God and mystical thoughts can only accomplish things that nature can already do on its own? Hmm. Odd, huh?

How much more could we accomplish as a society if we dealt in reality only? How much more could we achieve if we stopped pretending to do things by doing nothing at all? Imagine if all of us, or even most of us, thought realistically and logically, and tackled problems using actual solutions, rather than mimicking the thought processes of 7-year-olds playing superhero games.

Brent MacLean

<u>Disappearing Deities</u>

Christians. I have question for you. You keep telling me there's only one God. So.... all the other gods that God keeps mentioning in the Bible, the ones he's paranoid about people sneaking off and worshipping.... where'd they go?

Did they just... leave? Did your God kill them off? Where the heck did they go?

Don't You Dare Hurt My Feelings While I'm Killing People

The respect, shelter, and protection that you demand for your religious beliefs also justifies, shelters and protects the beliefs of extremists and religious terrorists. That's just how it works.

Why do so many believers get so bent out of shape when someone questions their beliefs? If they're so sure about their convictions they shouldn't be bothered by someone asking a few simple questions about their validity. (They might want to give the inquisitors some evidence too. That would actually clear things up pretty quick.) I mean, if someone says to me, "Hey, I heard you were an atheist. How come you don't believe in God?" I don't get upset. Not at all. I answer them. I give them my reasons (which just so happen to be based on thought, research, and logic). If someone asks why I believe present-day humans originated in Africa or why I unabashedly state that evolution is a fact, I don't feel hurt, threatened, or disrespected. I just answer the question. Philosopher Daniel Dennett has talked about how religious people have made it such that merely questioning religion is considered rude and impolite. Why is that? Why do their feelings get hurt so easily? How did we get here? How did we get to a place where people can make outrageous and unfounded claims about the most impossible of things, and expect, and often receive, the utmost respect? It's completely backwards. It flies in the face of everything progressive and rational. And why is rationality a bad thing? Why is asking questions so wrong? Just because an authority figure tells you something is true, you don't automatically believe it, do you? I made that mistake as a child. I trusted adults a bit too much. But I was a kid—I had an excuse. What's the excuse of all these gullible grownups that never think to question what they were taught about God and religion? I had a Christian woman flat-out tell me "You're not supposed to ask questions about God. You're just supposed to believe." Can you imagine telling your children that? Can you imagine telling your kids, "When someone tells you something that sounds unlikely or unbelievable do not question it. Just believe it." What a stagnant and frightening world that would be. Oh, the religious folk would love it. They'd love nothing more than for humans to learn nothing new about our universe, because they know the more we learn the less relevant their religious institutions become. The question is the mortal enemy of religion.

And let me ask you, Kind Believer, you believe we should respect everyone's beliefs, right? You believe that it's rude for someone like me to question a person that says God talks directly to them, correct? Because, who am I to say God didn't speak to this fellow? And I can't prove God *didn't* talk to him, right? Well, how about when God tells this guy that he needs to rid the world of infidels? How about when God tells this man that when he kills the heathens of the world he will be doing the Lord's work and will be rewarded in the afterlife?

Oh, you don't think God would say that? Well, who are *you* to question this man and his relationship with God? You can't prove God *didn't* tell this man to set off bombs in crowded parks and markets. Who are you to decide what God did and did not say to this man? Many believers I've talked to had problems with someone like me questioning their "personal relationship" with God. But I guarantee you these people would have no problem questioning Mr. Heathen Killer and *his* personal relationship with God. What it seems to boil down to is that no one can question *you* and *your* God but you can question others. You say it's different because God wouldn't instruct a man to do such awful things. Well, let me ask you, where did you get the idea that God is so good? Where does it say he would never do such things? A

18

while back I was having a conversation with a relative that was defending a man that claimed that God saved him from a mass shooting in a movie theater by persuading him to move to another seat, while a dozen other people were shot to death. I asked her why, if God was getting involved, he didn't stop the shooter from murdering people full stop. She said the shooter was acting on his own free will, and that God does not interfere with that. I pointed out that this person's opinion was contradictory, that she was saying that while God could and did save some people by influencing their actions, he could do nothing about the horrible actions of the gunman. I simply couldn't understand why God would save some people while letting others die, including children. I also couldn't understand why, if God was able to interfere and alter the events as they unfolded, why he couldn't do something to the shooter himself to stop the massacre from occurring in the first place. I didn't get any sensible answers, of course. Just the usual circular Christian response. But here's a funny thing. I noticed this woman kept saying, "But *I* believe God wouldn't do that..." and "But *I* believe God does help..." She was really putting an emphasis on the 'I', as if it added some sort of validity to her argument. So I asked her, "But where are you getting that?" She again started, "Well, *I* believe— "Again I said, "But where are you getting that?" She finally said, "From myself." I said, "So... you're making it up?" She said, "Uhhh. Yes."

She said yes! She admitted she was making up her own beliefs about God! And she wasn't the slightest bit embarrassed by the absurdity of it all.

Well, dear relative of mine, if you would have read your Bible you would have found out quite quickly that God orders more people to be killed than the Nazis and the Catholic Church combined. Seems to me you're just making up your own ideas about God's nature and expecting others to abide by your concept of what he is all about.

The bottom line is this: If we respect and protect religious beliefs the way we are expected to do so nowadays, then we must also respect the religious beliefs of those that believe differently than us. Whether or not they believe God tells them to harm others is beside the point, because the validity of a person's claim can never be challenged. Hey, you are the one that demanded that religious beliefs be protected and never critiqued. So the next time a bunch of guys hijack a plane because God wants them to kill thousands of people, make sure you don't ask them any questions about how they got to that conclusion, because that would be terribly rude.

<u>Everyone is Stupid for a Reason</u>

"Everything happens for a reason."

This is one of the worst sayings we have. Of course everything happens for a reason! The ball bounced because I dropped it. The puddle dried up because the water evaporated. The squirrel died because it had a heart attack. People most often use this phrase in relation to some bad situation. When I lost my job a few years ago I was talking to an employment preparation agent about what happened and how bad I felt. Attempting to console me she said, "Well, you know, everything happens for a reason." I appreciated the effort but it's just a really weird statement. I realize that what people like her actually mean is that everything happens for a *good* reason, and that everything will work out in the end. Quite often people invoke the religious angle and throw in "If God sees you to it God will see you through it" or some such thing. But really, it's just nonsense. Because I hate to tell you, but things don't always work out. Things don't always end up being "for the better" for people. Sometimes bad things just happen, and sometimes it leads to nothing good. And when that happens, who can I complain to? The people that use the stupid saying? God, for not seeing me through it? Besides, we all really know that everything doesn't happen for a good reason, with an ultimately good outcome. That's why no one chances it. We go to the doctor. We try to solve our own problems. We get help from others. We don't just trust everything to this silly notion of things working out for the best, and we certainly don't trust everything to God. The only ones that do are those nutty jerks you read about that prayed for their child's terminal illness to disappear, rather than seeking actual medical help. Recently when such a story was in the news a friend called the parents "sick bastards". As a tongue-in-cheek response I said, "They weren't sick. They were religious." A believer chimed in to state the obvious that those type folks don't define all believers. My response to that was, "Of course not. Luckily for children, most believers would never trust something so important as their child's health to God. He has a terrible track record when it comes to protecting kids." That was the end of the conversation. The believers had nothing more to say because they simply couldn't deny what I said. If they believe God answers prayers, they certainly would admit he doesn't answer them all, not even close, and thus they would have to admit that praying alone is pure insanity in such a situation. They would have to admit they know *they* need to take action, because whether or not they attribute the unfolding of things in life to God or not, they know that everything doesn't always work out, even if it does happen "for a reason". The saying is simply meaningless. And sometimes it's even harmful.

Don't believe me? Well, the next time you hear someone has cancer just reply with, "Well, everything happens for a reason," and see how well it goes over.

Evil or Religious? (Beliefs with a Twist)

I think to call Osama bin Laden evil is to completely miss the point of what he was all about. I recently said this to a few relatives. They seriously considered turning me in as a traitor to my country.

I will not claim to be an Osama bin Laden expert. But I've listened to many people who are and there seems to be a consensus that his beliefs, and subsequent actions based on those beliefs, were motivated by his love, fear, and devotion to God. Not only did he think he was doing what God wanted him to do— erase all infidels from the earth—he thought he would be punished if he didn't.

If you *truly believed* that the Almighty creator and ruler of the universe wanted you to do something, anything, and would punish you soundly if you refused, believe me, you would do it. This shouldn't be a hard concept to grasp, but it seems to be for most people, and I think I know why. It's because the religious folk here in the western world aren't true believers. They don't truly and wholeheartedly believe that God exists, and even more so, that any human has any idea what God wants from us even if he did. Oh, I'm sure there are a few idiots who believe they actually know the *essence* of God, but they are few and far between. Most likely they are already locked away in mental institutions or prisons. True believers would actually find it very hard to function in society.

For one, there are the countless contradictions in the Bible. For example: *Thou shalt not kill* vs. *"Go up, my warriors, and the land of Merathaim and against the people of Pekod. Yes, march against Babylon, the land of the rebels, a land that I will judge! Pursue, kill, and completely destroy them, as I have commanded*

23

you," says the LORD. (Jerimiah 50:21) And what about when God orders the death (by stoning) of the man that was gathering sticks on the Sabbath? Well, Mr. God, can we kill or not? How about all that love Jesus preached? What about, *If a man lies with a man as with a woman, both of them shall be put to death for their abominable deed; they have forfeited their lives.(Leviticus 20:13)*? That doesn't sound all that loving to me. So to be a literal believer of the Good Book you'd have to do and believe one thing while doing and believing the exact opposite. It's impossible. Not to mention all the stuff that is provably inaccurate in that silly book. But most believers are not literalists. Most are casual believers. Religious moderates.

It's actually a simple thing to figure out whether or not you *truly believe* that God's followers go to heaven for eternity while bad people go to hell for roughly the same time period. If one truly believes that if they don't follow the basic tenets of the faith that God will send them to hell forever, one would not even risk breaking those rules. Seriously, if I believed that if I stole something (Thou shalt not steal—a basic commandment given to Moses by God himself) I would most definitely burn in hell for all eternity, you'd better believe I wouldn't have bought a cable splitter so I could have cable in the bedroom too. No matter how much I enjoy lying in bed and watching TV it would certainly not be worth risking an eternity burning in the lake of fire. The reality of it is that even the people that claim to be true believers have doubts. Serious doubts. Many will not even entertain such an idea but it's true. And if you count yourself as a true Christian but don't even follow the basic tenets that God and his crew laid out for everyone, well then you aren't a *true* believer and you're just focusing on what you want to be important, so that no matter how you look at it, you're *just good enough* to get into heaven. That's what most people do.

Before I go too far off point here I want to share with you

what Tony Soprano said about heaven and hell. Yes, I know he's a fictional character but his thoughts on the topic are pretty typical, even if his exact circumstances were anything but. He said that he, the boss of a mafia crime family, was not the type of person that would go to hell. He was a crook, a thief, an adulterer, a gangster, a murderer. Yet he felt he wouldn't go to hell because hell is reserved for "the worst people. The Hitler's, the Pol Pot's. The sick and degenerate fucks that torture and kill little kids." If you asked the average believer, the religious moderate, if they thought they were going to end up in hell, nine times out of ten they would say no, even though, if they were being honest, they would have to admit to not actually obeying the rules that must be followed to keep you out of Satan's gated community. There's a lot of cherry-picking in religion, no doubt about it. It's pretty much just people deciding what to believe, which is, as I've stated before, an impossible act. You cannot choose your beliefs. If you could it would be simple enough for you to decide to believe, right now as you're reading this, that 2+2=5. But you can't do that. Your mind won't let you. Logic gets in the way. You can only choose what to hope for, and what to actively follow. I think this is an important statement worth typing again. *You don't choose what to believe. You can only choose what to hope for and what to actively follow.*

So given that Osama bin Laden seems to have been one of those rare people that actually believed in this shit (except Islam's shit rather than Christianity's), it's not surprising to me that he would be so extreme. The few people that truly believe *are* the extreme ones. Why do you think they're called extremists? He was doing anything and everything he could to make certain he didn't end up on God's bad side, eternally punished for disobedience. In his eyes, bin Laden was simply a loyal follower of God. His actions were evil but he was not. He was religious; truly religious. To be evil is to inflict harm upon other for the sake of inflicting harm, to watch and revel in the suffering of innocents. Well, to bin Laden and the thousands of people that share his beliefs, we are not innocents. *We* are the evil ones, infecting the earth with our ungodly ways. He was doing God's work—harsh and extreme acts that God commanded him to do.

[Please bear with me while I take a moment for the necessary disclaimer: I don't like Osama bin Laden. I didn't support him or his organization, I didn't agree with any of his beliefs or ideals, and I'm glad he was killed. I mean, really. I hate Christianity, so you can imagine how I feel about Islam. This post is simply to say that I do not believe that he was necessarily evil.]

No, I don't call him evil. But I do call him insane. He was insane in the sense that he believed in strange fairy tales and far-fetched ideas about time, space, existence, and the afterlife. I believe that is a mental problem. But it happens to be a problem that most people cherish and protect. We pretend that belief— blind faith—is some kind of virtue. You've heard it before. When some person does something horrible the neighbours always say, "Jeez, I just can't believe he did that. He was always such a nice guy; friendly, helpful, church-going man..." as if that makes the person more refined, respectable, and civilized. (I think it's quite funny to call someone that claims to live their life according to a Bronze Age text 'civilized'.) We pretend that believing in these ridiculous notions makes perfect sense. We honour and respect and protect these beliefs. But what so many don't seem to get is that when you protect and encourage such unwarranted and unbelievable beliefs, it's inevitable that you'll soon start seeing other people with the same unwarranted and unbelievable beliefs, *but with a twist!* With their own interpretation, their own subjective slant; their own *violent* slant. And you can't say, "Hey! That twist you put on your beliefs, that's not nice! That's not what *we* believe! God isn't telling you those things!" because your new adversary can simply reply, "Hey! You can't prove that God didn't tell me these things! I think *you're* wrong about how *you* interpret the words! And I don't think God is telling *you* the things you claim he does!" See, once you start validating beliefs unsupported by evidence, all is fair in this game of wacky ideas. And all of a sudden you have a religious disagreement, which sometimes leads to religious wars. And whether you simply disagree with one another or you're killing one another you're both on equal ground. Shaky ground, yes, but equal nonetheless. You both have the same amount of proof (pretty close to none, as it were) and you both have to accept each other's side if you want your own to be protected from scrutiny. And therein lies the problem.

Who says God didn't tell Osama bin Laden to wipe America and Israel from the map? You can't call him on that crazy bullshit because you didn't call George W. Bush on his "God wanted me to be president" and "God told me to invade Iraq" nonsense. Both of these men were doing God's work, in their respective opinions, and you simply cannot restrict one person's unfounded belief while protecting another's and have any credibility. The *only* way you can invalidate one and validate the other is by doing something crazy like using empirical evidence to prove the likelihood or unlikelihood of a given claim. It's what we do with everything. Well, everything except religion.

Either we encourage people to follow their unsupported beliefs or we don't. There's really no middle ground. You can say the line is crossed when it involves hurting or killing people, but the person doing the hurting and killing can simply say, "This is what God told me to do. Who are you to question God the Almighty?" And he would be correct. If we are to follow the groundwork we've already laid we cannot question anyone doing God's work, even if that work is heinous and deadly, because you can't prove God didn't tell him to do these things. See? There's that old 'proving a negative' thing again. (All you "atheists can't prove God don't exist" people know this little fallacy well. I'm

27

sure you see the lack of logic now that I've applied it to your own contention.)

People, it's all equally insane. One side just happens to be more destructive than the other at this moment in history. (Although, again, they would make the argument that the infidels have done much more damage than they have, but whatever. That's neither here nor there for the point I'm trying to make.) But what's interesting to me is that if you take out the killing that's so prevalent in bin Laden's deeds, his beliefs are no crazier than the beliefs people have over here. They might be uglier in that he put them into action, but they are no less likely to be true. They are no less valid when it comes to what *is* and what *is not*.

There's an invisible man in the sky? Check.

He's the creator of all time and space? Check.

He has an insatiable and insecure need to be loved and adored? Check.

He has commandments and rules that determine one's eligibility into an awesome afterlife? Check.

He has commandments and rules that, if not followed, will lead to entry into a horrible eternity of pain and suffering? Check.

We are all safe from having to provide evidence for these claims about His existence, and His restrictions and instructions? Check*MATE!*

Both sides share all these things. As much as people on this side of the world want to deny it, orders to kill the unholy exist in the Christian Bible as well. The difference is that

Christians don't act upon them.

Why? Because they don't truly believe. And thank God for that.

Far From Automatic

Comedian Adam Carolla said, "I'm not bothered that these imbeciles buy into it; I'm bothered that we as a society give them such a wide berth." How many times have I said something quite similar to this? It's endlessly disappointing when religious moderates and atheists alike pander to the religious, whether it be out of fear of offending them, or simply because they think "that's the way things are; that's how we treat religion, we respect it wholeheartedly." Again and again I find myself having to say it: respecting the right to believe something is fine, but respecting the belief itself is far from automatic. For instance, people that believe that homosexuality is "unnatural" are morons, or at the very least, ignorant, when it comes to nature. The people that believe homosexuality is a choice, those people are morons too. The people that believe it's an "abomination" and an affront to God and "a threat to family life and the institution of marriage" when two people of the same sex marry are idiots. I feel no apprehension in saying these things. Those beliefs are horrible and do not deserve my respect.

But again, I'm not telling you folks to call people morons. I'm suggesting that you stand up for what's decent and stop protecting the aspects of people's beliefs that you know are unfair, cruel, and prejudicial. Make a small stand, that's all. You don't need to become a raging atheist or a great crusader for anything. But rather than giving the stock answer "I don't agree but I respect your beliefs", say "I'm sorry but you're wrong about that." Why not tell them that all humans are equal and all deserve the right to love who they love and marry who they want to marry? Why not tell them they have no right to decide for other people what's right for them when it comes to love and relationships?

Why not tell them that homosexuality is a natural thing that happens all throughout nature, in countless species of animal?

Can you imagine how much further along we'd be as a society if regular people stood up for what's right rather than cowering at the feet of someone that uses the word "religion" as a shield for their unfounded and discriminatory beliefs? Think about it. Think about what it would be like if we never shied away from critiquing things that desperately need critiquing. Think about all the people that wouldn't have had to live in fear of offending the beliefs of someone that never has to explain or rationalize their oppressive opinions. Think about the freedom people could have if religious beliefs of others weren't used to ridicule, shame, and even subjugate them. Isn't that alone reason enough to cease this protection of harmful belief systems? Isn't that reason enough to speak up when someone is spouting such harmful decrees?

The Father, the Son, and the Holy Grandfather

The reasoning is so simple, isn't it? It's the reasoning that even a child possesses. This is an actual conversation I had with a friend when I was about 6 years old:

Me: "So God made the world, everything."

Friend: "Yup. Everything. The universe."

Me: "So where did God come from?"

Friend: "He just always was. He was always there."

Me: "He had to have a beginning."

Friend: "Nope. He always was."

Turns out this isn't just some little boy making up his own nonsensical answers; this is what millions of adults believe! Now, I could ask questions like "what was God doing for all that time?" because, after all, we're talking about eternity here. So if you take away the time he allotted for us, whether it be 6000 years for you Bible-crazy history-deniers, or 4.54 billion years (for the earth, not humans) for you people that are partial to proven facts, the time before us and/or earth is still pretty much eternity. We haven't used up *one billionth of a percent* of God's time, not even close. So what was God doing? Was he alone all that time? Did he create other universes and other people? I could ask these questions, but I won't. I'll stick to the original point here, which is the idea of "the watchmaker".

"The watch had to have a watchmaker," they say. The contention is that the workings are so intricate and complicated that they had to have a designer. How could this world, with its rich and diverse systems of life, have existed without such an intelligent 'creator'? Okay, fine. Let's go with that logic, even though it's a little flawed. Let's say that everything that exists had to have had a maker, especially evident when things are complicated, multifaceted, or intricate. Wouldn't you then agree that God, whatever he is, must also be pretty complicated and multifaceted? Surely you would agree that such a being with the ability to create the universe is certainly more complicated than a simple watch. So it may not surprise you that the next question is: So who made God? Who designed such an amazing entity? He couldn't have just "always been" because, as we have already agreed, something that works so well, something so magnificent as a watch, must have been created by someone or something intelligent. So who designed the fantastic being that designed us? Who created our creator? Maybe it wasn't an act of creation such as a watchmaker making a watch. Maybe it was more like the creation of a baby; kind of an automatic occurrence after some sort of interaction between two separate beings. If so, my next question naturally is: Who are God's parents? Did someone give birth to God? Were two beings needed, like male and female human beings that come together to create a baby? And if two male and female-like beings did create God—if God has a dad—shouldn't we be worshipping *him?* (I'm not going to suggest we worship God's mom because I'm aware how little world religions think of women.) I mean this guy created God! Surely that's worth adoration and awe. To create such a thing as God, I mean, wow. If he didn't create our God our God wouldn't have created us! We're ignoring the real talent here! It's like we're busy wasting time watching God on *Hawaii Five-0* when we should be

33

appreciating his dad's amazing work in *The Godfather*.

We worship and adore God because he created us. So does he in turn worship and adore the one who created him? Does he worship his God? Is that why God lets this world suffer through such terrible tragedies like cancer and tsunamis? Is that why he lets little girls get raped and murdered? Is that why starvation is rampant and genocide is still not uncommon? Is that why women are still oppressed and treated worse than cattle in many parts of the world? Is it simply because he's busy worshipping *his* creator? Is he as fixated on praising his God as many of us seem to be with ours? Are people praying to God while he's praying to his? Maybe that's why prayers so often go unanswered. God's busy. He's busy praying. I wonder if any of *his* prayers get answered. Probably not. God's God is probably busy himself, praying to the God that created him. Because surely a being so intelligent and complex that it can create a God that is so intelligent and complex that it can create our universe *must* have had a creator. Right?

Fizzling, Dwindling, and Dying a Beneficial Death

You may think from the sarcastic and irritated tone of some of my writing that I go around trying to convince people to turn their back on their religion and to stop believing in God and ghosts and psychics and such. I do no such thing. I won't lie, I think it would be awesome if people became more critical and questioned such things. I believe it would better humankind as a whole. But no, I do not go around ripping people's beliefs down. That is unless I'm challenged. But even then it never lasts. Conversations with believers are almost always short. Why? Because they run out of excuses real quick and/or they get offended and angry. But I must admit that these conversations and debates have grown tiresome. I'm just repeating the same things over and over; things I think mature adults should be able to come up with on their own. I mean, why not? I did, and I'm not particularly intelligent. No one ever tried to convince me to be an atheist. It's just a natural conclusion to rational thinking.

So no, I don't automatically criticize people for their beliefs no matter how silly they are. There's no point. Over time I've learned (and I wish I learned it sooner) that the people that want to believe in nonsense will believe in nonsense (or at least say and act like they do), and people that are interested in facts, what is and what is not, will ask questions and be happy to discuss things, and often be elated if you open their eyes to something new. There's still nothing that excites me more than a radical new idea I never considered before—especially one that stands up through inquiry and scrutiny.

I've been baited into religious conversations before, and I used to go in full-on, guns blazing. I now know that's not a good idea. You really gotta pick your spots if you want to remain in good standing with the people involved. As crazy as it sounds some people will hate you simply for being an atheist, and that's something I never dreamed possible. I've written before about a place where I once worked where they ridiculed me for being a nonbeliever. I didn't really mind though, because at that time I was more than happy to shoot them down with rationality and reason. But now I realize that wasn't how I should have handled it. I learned once they canned me (yep, they did) that I shouldn't think that just because a person brings up a topic it means they are cool with discussing it. Weird but true. Sometimes it's just for the purposes of junior high-type ridicule.

Recently a friend was telling me about a woman we both know and how she has developed an interest in religion. She's starting to ask questions and admits that it lacks logic. She knows of my interest in the subject and asked (through the mutual friend) if I would lend her a few books on the topic. I told the mutual friend that I don't think I will. Why? Because I've spoken to this woman. I've been around her during the death of a mutual relative. I saw how she reacted, heard the things she said, and to be honest, I don't think she's really ready. That's not for me to judge, I know, but I don't want to be responsible for someone losing their faith when they really want it, or even need it. Not like that. I want people to *want* to know. That's the key. I asked our mutual friend, "Does she really want to know? Is she actually interested in finding out what religion is all about?" Nowadays, if I find myself engaged in a conversation with a believer I ask them, "If there were no God, would you even want to know?" Another time a friend was at my house and asked if he could borrow my copy of *The God Delusion* by Richard Dawkins. After asking him a few questions I realized he was indeed a believer and even prayed every night. I advised him not to take the book. He's a great guy and I know how these things can go; I didn't want to risk the friendship. He insisted he really wanted to read it. I told him to just be prepared for having his faith shaken. It wasn't a definite thing, of course, but there was a pretty good chance that that might happen. He assured me he was okay with that. He took the book. I don't really know what he thought of it; we never really discussed it. All he said to me about it was that he no longer prayed every night.

Yes, I'd love for everyone in the world to drop every silly superstition they have. I'd love for everyone to call bullshit on the priests, ministers, and imams who claim to have answers they know they don't have. I'd love for people to stop believing in the fairy tales from that immoral Bronze Age text you find in every hotel room nightstand. Perhaps most of all, I'd love for people to be able to say, "I don't know." What I don't want is to rip apart individual people, good and decent people, and take away something they need. Is it sad that they need it? I think so. Is it a sign of weakness? I think so. But I'm not going to take advantage of that weakness. There are thousands of books and websites to consult if they're interested. If they really want to talk to me about such things they can read this blog or talk to me directly. But I would first want to know if they are truly interested and open to the possibility of having their mind changed. As I said earlier, it's not a definite thing anyway. But if they are open to a new way of looking at it all, a critical and realistic way of thinking, I'd like nothing more than to be a part of it. And who knows, even if they give me all the time in the world I still might not change their minds one iota. The important thing is that they—all of us—are open to the *possibility*.

So how do I hope the world gets rid of religion? The youth. It must be filtered out through the inquisitive minds of the youth. That's how it has to happen. I hope parents no longer force their baseless beliefs upon their children. I hope they teach their children to think critically. I hope they stop baptizing babies and

37

forcing adolescents to go through that ridiculous 'confirmation' process. I hope they stop branding small children as Christians, Jews, and Muslims when the child is far too young to understand the concept. The child doesn't know. The child didn't decide. And to the ones that do have parents that saddle them with religious affiliation of some sort, I hope they grow to see the hypocritical nonsense of their parents, and eventually the superstitions of old will all but disappear. I've heard some people call religion a virus. That's exactly what it is. It's the same as racism, sexism, or any kind of nonsensical and irrational mode of thought. It's passed down from generation to generation. And I'm not naïve enough to think it will ever completely go away. Not even close. But I do think it's possible for the civilized world to come to a point where religion is not a given, and it's not protected from the scrutiny it so severely deserves. No, as long as there are people there will be religion. This I'm sure. But it is fizzling in our ever-progressing culture. It's dwindling. It's dying. And that is surely a death that would benefit the world in ways we could never imagine.

For Goodness' Sake. Not God's

Consider these two statements:

Statement #1: I'm not going to hurt that person because God will punish me if I do.

Statement #2: I'm not going to hurt that person because I don't want that person to hurt and I certainly don't want to be responsible for their pain.

Those two sentences sum up a major disparity between believers and non-believers. Every vocal atheist has heard it: "Well, if you don't believe in God or the Bible where do you get your morals? How do you know right from wrong?"

Those questions tell you a lot about the person asking them. First, it tells you that they're not very knowledgeable about the Bible or God. Because if they were they would know that God instructs us to do some pretty evil shit for the flimsiest of reasons. There's a lot of stoning ordered by God. Countless men, women, and children are slaughtered under direct instruction from the Man Upstairs. And if they have read the Bible and still think it's a great manual on how to live a good and moral life then they are simply cherry-picking. (Christians really love those cherries!) They're ignoring all the bad parts and citing the nice bits for their own use, which is a very dishonourable way to form an argument, if you ask me.

Second, the "where do you get your morals?" question tells you there's not much keeping this person from robbing you right now. They're only *not* robbing you (or worse) because they're afraid of what God might think. They, alone, by themselves, without God, would be *without* morals, and would have no qualms about doing pretty much whatever they want no matter who gets hurt.

Of course, I know that's not true. I don't believe that these people are evil folks who are only not murdering people because they are afraid of punishment in the afterlife. But that is exactly what their argument supposes.

So where do I get my morals? Mostly from myself, from my own mind. I think morals are linked to genetics somehow, meaning that in an evolutionary sense it's beneficial for survival to be good to other people. I can't prove that but I've read some articles where scientists suggest that very thing. Of course, some of it has to do with how a person was raised. It's nature and nurture, that old story. But I can tell you this. I certainly don't have my morals because I'm afraid of being punished if I don't do good things. To suggest such a thing is actually insulting. If you imply that the only reason I'm not a bad person doing bad things is for fear of pissing off an invisible man in the sky, well, then you're basically saying that I'm not a good person. You're saying I'm only doing good things out of *fear*; fear of missing out on heaven and fear of ending up in hell. I don't like hurting others. Hell, I don't even like inconveniencing other people. Does that make me special? No. It just means I'm a person with morals that do not come from fear of punishment or hope of reward. There's a huge difference. Doing good things because you're afraid of hell and want to be rewarded (in heaven) is a terrible reason to do good things. It's like giving to charity only when you know you'll get rewarded for it later. It ruins the spirit of it. The meaning is lost. The morality is absent. The deed might be good but the motivation is selfish.

Read the two sentences at the top of this post again. Which statement sounds more moral? With all things being equal, and you only have these two statements to go on, which person is the better one, ethically? Which person is doing good things because they *are* good and which is doing it for personal gain?

I know the answer. And so do you. The question is whether or not you accept the real answer, or pick the one that suits your needs.

God Guide This Ham

Don't you find these Christian athletes annoying? I'm not talking about athletes that just happen to be believers. I'm talking about the people that thank God after a touchdown or thank Jesus after a win. It's irritating and insulting. Insulting to whom? Why, to God, of course.

These Christians are implying that God actually cares who gets the next goal, scores the final point, and gets the win, and that he even intervenes in how these sporting events play out. And that implies that God cares more about fixing the Superbowl than saving three year old Chloe from the cancer that's spreading through her body. And that implies God is a heartless prick with fucked up priorities.

Hey God, instead of guiding the ball gently into the hands of the wide receiver, why not guide a ham into the hands of a mother whose children are starving to death?

God's Nuts!

What's the main reason I do not believe in intelligent design? The human penis.

No *intelligent* being would ever design such a thing. But Christians think that "God made man in his own image". I actually think that's just another instance of human arrogance, coupled with a stunning lack of imagination. But that's nothing new. Anyway, considering we're made in his image I have a few questions about God then. Ready?

Does God have testicles? He must because we have them and we were made in his image. So *why* does God have testicles? He must have a penis too. Well, why does he have a penis? Either he is urinating, having sex (for pleasure, procreation, or both), masturbating, or a combination of these things. Why else would he have genitalia?

What about a belly button? Skeptics have asked that very question about Adam too. Why would Adam, who didn't have a mother, need a belly button, which is where the umbilical cord connects to the baby so the mother can feed him while he is in her womb? So I ask it too, of Adam *and* God. Why would God need a belly button? And is he an inny or an outie? Gotta be an inny. Outie's are gross In fact, I hate belly buttons altogether. I hate knowing I have one. But that's another blog post.

Nipples. Many people ask why men have them. They say they are pointless on a man. Either way, they do have them, so one has to assume that God has nipples too. Why? Why does God have nipples? Why does God have a body at all? If he is the only God there is, which Christians seem to think (monotheism is a concept I never quite understood—why would there only be one lonely God up there?) then why does he have a body? You mean he's just a man.... somewhere.... all alone? So what does he do with his time?

Does God have an ass? He must if we were made in his image. Sooooo... does he produce..... excrement? Why else would one have an ass? (I could go into a *God might be a homosexual* concept here.... but.... nah.) I guess this also means God eats food. What kind? Where does it come from? Does he just make his favourite foods appear? Can he make it so that he doesn't need to eat food in the first place? Is he that powerful? Can he make it so he can be nourished without the digestion process, thus eliminating the need for an ass altogether? Is God so powerful he can make his own ass disappear?

Okay, obviously this could go on forever. That's one thing about God. Once you ask a question it inevitably leads to more. And the funniest part is that no one—*no one!*—has any of the answers.

The Great Credit Hog in the Sky

This is a short back-and-forth between me and some lady in the comments section under a video about a boy that was bullied to the point of considering suicide.

Lady: "And there is a God, something kept that boy from killing himself... the million reasons why he didn't, that's a perfect example right there. And all these comments about there is no God'. You have to believe in a God to believe there isn't a God."

Me: "You wrote 'And all these comments about "there is no God". You have to believe in a God to believe there isn't a God.' That comment is so good I have to blog about it. I suppose I have to believe in leprechauns to believe there are no leprechauns too, right? You also say, 'Something kept that boy from killing himself.' I agree. *He* did. He did with his own strength and courage. And we should commend him for it, rather than give the credit to someone else."

This tendency to attribute every good event to God is friggin' annoying. She beat cancer? That was God's doing. He survived the crash? God saved him. She found her sunglasses even though she left them on a bench in a crowded park? The Almighty protected those shades, damn it.

Look, sometimes good stuff happens and sometimes bad stuff happens. That's life. But these people contend that everything good is from God, which means everything bad is because of... Satan... I guess? Well, sometimes it's Satan, other times it's just evil humans. What a strange assumption based on nothing at all. It's annoying in and of itself, but I think it gets downright insulting when someone like this boy uses his own strength, intelligence, and courage to overcome something, to get through some kind of hardship, and people credit God. No! Credit the boy! *He's* the one that got through it! It's the same thing when doctors save someone's life and people thank God. Thank the doctors! They were the ones that reattached Sammy's head. If God was so great he would have stopped the hippo from biting it off in the first place, no?

And while we're on the subject, when you're busy screaming that it was a miracle that your friend got the kidney or liver they so desperately needed, keep in mind that on the other end there is a family mourning the death of a loved one. I'm pretty sure they'd appreciate you not referring to it as a "miracle".

<u>The Greatest Lie Ever Told</u>

We recently found out we are going to have a baby, and someone asked me if I was going to "teach atheism" to my child. I couldn't help but laugh. You don't really "teach atheism". Atheism just is. It's automatic. Everyone is born an atheist. You don't start believing in god-myths until the people around you convince you of it. Conversely, science, and the scientific method, is automatic if one considers what's real about the world around them. Magician Penn Jillette said:

> If every trace of any single religion was wiped out and nothing was passed on, it would never be created exactly that way again. There might be some other nonsense in its place, but not that exact nonsense. If all of science were wiped out, it would still be true and someone would find a way to figure it all out again.

The only time you have to "teach atheism" it is when someone has already been brainwashed by superstitions. And even then you're not really teaching it; you're encouraging critical thought and fact-based knowledge. Teaching atheism. It's just a strange phrase. Imagine my child is fours year old and I look at him and say, "Ringo, there is no God, okay?" and sweet little Ringo looks at me and says, "But dear father, what's a God?" That's exactly what would happen if the superstitious nonsense spouted by others wasn't rampant. Ringo wouldn't automatically believe in any gods. He'd probably just start asking questions, which is exactly what we all should be doing. But no, we let priests and popes and pastors and relatives, who pretend to have all the answers, pollute our kids' minds with silly old myths. No, let's

Brent MacLean

listen to all those people about the nature of the world rather that the brilliant biologists and physicists that are actually *figuring out* the world around us. No, I'm sure your Nana knows more about where humans came from and how the universe came into existence.

But I will say this: If my precious little Ringo comes home from school and tells me his classmates (or worse—much worse—his teacher) told him there is a God and he's watching all of us and if we do anything he doesn't like he will send us to hell to burn forever and yada yada yada... you better believe I will tell him the truth: "It's all lies, Ringo. It's just old stories from long ago when people didn't know as much about the world as we do now. Some people still believe it, but it's just not true."

I don't want to lie to my child about it. I don't want to contribute to this bullshit. I like facts and truth and reason. I'm not baptizing my child and saddling him with a religious affiliation before he can say a single word. I would never send my child to a religious school. I have heard atheist parents justify this very thing by saying, "Well, when he gets older he can decide for himself." That amazes me. They obviously know very little about the binding grip of real faith. It can be tight, man, so tight it never lets go. When it comes to growing into a reasonable adult, you're already ensuring your child begins way behind the starting line. You're making it more likely that your child will eventually face a mental and emotional uphill battle because you are afraid of the truth, afraid of not being politically correct, afraid of upsetting religious people. Talk about sacrificing your son! And no, it's not a definite thing. My wife grew up around the church and partook in church-related activities, with a moderately religious family. Yet she felt no fear as a child and had no problem declaring herself an atheist as a young adult; something she did years before I did. Strangely enough, my family wasn't religious at all and I didn't attend church, except for religious holidays when my

48

school would make all the kids go. We had a few Bibles in our house, but no one read them. We did however have a big illustrated "Children's Bible" that my parents gave to my older brother when he was a baby. That book absolutely fascinated me. Even now I can vividly picture so many of the illustrations that so captivated me. There was a giant golden statue that a group of people were worshipping; there was the creation scene, with all the trees and animals. (And yes, in case you're wondering, there were brontosauruses in the Garden of Eden). There was a lovely depiction of Eve handing Adam an apple while a snake slithers in a tree behind her. (I guess the illustrators weren't aware that nowhere in the Genesis tale is there an apple. That's right. It says fruit, not apple.) But the pictures that stood out the most were ones like the three boys standing in a pit of fire. Engulfed in flames they stood there confidently, some might say smugly, because they were being protected from the flames by God. I remember wondering what that would be like and how good you had to be for God to make you flame retardant. And then there was the devil. That picture freaked me out. It was the scene where Satan tempts Jesus and Jesus tells him to get lost. Jesus stands atop a hill; arms outstretched and face to the sky, while Lucifer seems to be flying away, cast away, as it were. Now when I imagine that devil he looks sort of like a villain in a superhero movie. But in my child's mind he looked like the epitome of evil. He had horns, of course. And he had what looked like a cape, dramatically caught in the wind as he fled the Lord and Saviour. Besides the horns, he actually looked like a man for the most part. Except for those feet. God damn, those feet. They were hooves. Cloven hooves. I have no idea why but those hooves gave me the creeps.

I'm coming close to going off on a tangent here, but in a way it's not a tangent at all; more of an illustration of where my mind was at when I was a kid. My family was not a religious family, yet I believed the tidbits I read and heard. My brother would tell me things, about God and the 10 Commandments and such. (Plus he would "summon" the devil, assuring me the Dark One would appear at my bedside later that night. Standard stuff for older brothers, I suppose.) I would pay attention to what we learned in school, through the prayers we said every morning to the religious songs we sang at Christmas. For some reason I believed it all. Gullible, I suppose. But I was a kid, so maybe 'trusting' would be a better way to describe it. I simply believed that adults knew what they were talking about, and would never lie when it came to such important matters like God, heaven, death, and my eternal soul. My wife thinks it's strange, how much I thought about that stuff as a child. But I think 'How could I not?!' She says she just never thought about any of it, even though it was around her. And even though I wasn't in a particularly religious atmosphere, I got sucked in. I was a believer. And you better believe it wasn't easy getting to where I am now. I sometimes get messages from people that were brought up in very religious families. They've told me about the mental torture they've endured while engulfed in the faith, but even more so while getting away from it. I can only imagine how hard that must be. Given my apparent gullibility to such matters when I was young, I wonder if I had grown up in a really religious family, would I have ever gotten away from it. It wasn't even pounded into my head and still I was hooked. And scared. I was thinking about things that were far too heavy for my young mind. (Maybe someday I'll tell you about the Pentecostal Church play I attended as a child and how much it messed me up. I remember that day vividly—the play and what came afterward. It was too much for me, the guilt and the fear. I won't get into it in this post, the state I was in after being in that church. Just picture a little boy riding his bike in the pouring rain, pleading with God to understand that he was *trying* to be a good boy, he really was, but it just didn't seem like enough. I was too young to have that shit weighing on my mind. **No child** should ever enter a Pentecostal Church. Terrible, terrifying place.)

I'm proof that you don't have to be Nedward Flanders to mess your kids up with this stuff. When it comes to children from non-religious families that still get fed this garbage, or even worse, go to religious schools, even if they are lucky enough to grow up and develop a mind that reasons things through, they will still have the burden of first having to shed the greatest lie ever told. And that can be an impossible lie to break through. The guilt, the fear—it can be crushing. Look around you. Look at how many people never got out from under that superstitious weight. You got out? Good. But what if your child doesn't? It wasn't an easy road for me, a boy from a non-religious family. If I had been indoctrinated by a religious school too, and had to withstand the lies throughout my adolescence, who knows, I might never have allowed myself the freedom of thought that led to the realization that what everyone was telling me just made no sense. Why would you even risk such a thing with your own child? Why would you chance it and allow your child to be indoctrinated while you stand aside and hope they someday "figure it out" on their own?

I know far too many people that agree with most of what I say about religion yet still go along with things like baptisms, confirmations, and church weddings. Why? Why just follow along because everyone else does it? Is that a good thing to teach your kids? To do something because everyone else does? Stop being afraid of your parents. Those are the excuses I most often hear and I think they're pretty weak. Stand up for yourself. Even more, stand up for your children. Protect them. If you can save them from a lifetime of confusion, guilt, and emotional torment by simply being honest with them about religion, why wouldn't you do so?

Brent MacLean

<u>The Greeting Wars</u>

Happy Holidays!

It seems every year more and more people are taking offense to that phrase. (There are other slogans that are giving people grief as well. Season's Greetings, for instance. To keep things from getting convoluted I'm going to focus on one, Happy Holidays, in this post.) I hear the complaints on television and I've seen them posted on Facebook. The complainants seem to feel that to utilize this abhorrent phrase is to spit directly into the face of baby Jesus. The theory is that the phrase gained popularity because, as the world became more and more politically correct, people became afraid that saying "Merry Christmas" would offend people that weren't Christians. So over time Merry Christmas got replaced with Happy Holidays. Of course, the truth is you still see and hear Merry Christmas everywhere—it's not as if it's been banned—but enough Happy Holidays have popped up to make some Godly people angry, giving them something else to whine about.

What these people don't seem to understand is that the few—and it was indeed just a few—businesses that made the switch from one greeting to another really did it as a marketing maneuver, not a religious one. But I'm not going to talk much about that aspect of it anyway, because that would only address *why* the change actually occurred and not the underlying reason the change became an issue. The paranoia came before the commercial concerns, is what I mean. So I'm just going to attempt to clear up this whole debate right here and now, just for you, Silent Reader.

The people complaining—and I mean the people on both sides—are morons. In the first place, no one was upset because the words Merry Christmas were posted on walls. Nor was anyone offended because someone used Merry Christmas as a friendly greeting. And in the extremely unlikely event that there was a person that got angry over those two words, I'm sure it was one in a million and, well, I'm going to suggest, that the angry person was severely mentally ill. I'm not kidding. If anyone, any time, ever got upset because someone said Merry Christmas to them then they are insane. Plain and simple. I don't care what your religious beliefs are, whether you're a believer or an atheist, a Muslim or a Mennonite, or what your views are on the holiday itself. Why would anyone be mad about it? It's Christmas! We gotta pretend it isn't? Imagine someone says Merry Christmas to me, and I, not being a Christian, respond with, "How *dare* you? I'm not *Christian*." That would make me a god damn lunatic. Look, I'd love to live in a world where it's not assumed that I'm delusional enough to be a Christian. That would be awesome. But that's just not how it is. If someone assumes I celebrate Christmas and that I do so because I think Jesus is cool as shit, I don't care. And would someone really say, "Hey! I'm a Muslim! I'm offended by that Merry Christmas!"? Again, that would be insanity. The Muslim (or whomever) should respond with, "Merry Christmas to you too" or something along those lines. If I was in Israel and someone said Happy Hanukkah to me I wouldn't care either. I'm in a place that celebrates Hanukkah, so naturally I should expect to hear about it. If I'm in a country that celebrates Beyhanna, and a fellow at the market says, "Good day, and have a Happy Beyhanna!" I'm gonna thank him and say, "Same to you."

Have I said Merry Christmas to people? Absolutely. Not a lot, I'll admit, but that's due to shyness and nothing more. I've said it though and I have because it's Christmas! That's what you say! And saying Merry Christmas does not mean you're declaring a belief in God, Jesus, or Santa. You're not passing yourself off as devout. You're passing yourself off as polite. It's just another way of saying, "have a good day" or "see ya later" or "take care". It's a season-specific greeting.

As for you "Keep the Christ in Christmas" anti-Happy Holidays people, you're just as moronic as the folks you complain about. Suddenly saying Happy Holidays is akin to shouting, "Jesus touches little boys!"? Who cares if someone says Happy Holidays? Sometimes the people you hear using that phrase are forced to by their employer. And I would wager that 99% of the other people that say it are just saying it without much thought. They're certainly not making any attempt at political correctness, and they're definitely not making any stand against Christmas. It's more about a business making an attempt to be inclusive. They realize that not all of their patrons are Christians, so they use this all-enveloping, generic greeting. It doesn't mean they're trying to erase your favourite holiday, you fools. They're just trying to include everyone's favourite holiday. They're just saying a few harmless words. Stop being so sensitive all the time, seriously. Believe in *your* beliefs and leave the rest of us the hell alone, will ya? No one is going to take your Christmas away, and no one is trying to. Don't act like you're the only one celebrating Christmas "correctly". There is no correct way to celebrate Christmas. There are no rules. Different countries have different Christmas traditions and none of them are wrong. It's the same with you and your neighbours. You might have slightly different traditions but neither of you are doing it wrong. That goes for greetings as well. There's no wrong, just different. If you ask a dozen people to specify what the "true meaning" of Christmas is you will probably get as many answers. Again, none of them are wrong. Let's not forget that Christmas is actually a stolen holiday in the first place. It was a pagan Winter Solstice celebration that was around long before Jesus and Christianity. That's right, Christmas is a rip-off. But still, who cares? I don't. Christmas is a holiday where we eat a lot, visit relatives in an obligatory fashion while pretending we'd be visiting them even if it wasn't Christmas, and buy things for rich people that don't really need anything. It's not just about love and giving, as many people try to claim. It's about alcohol, time away from work and school, seeing the family, and the obligation of gift-giving. It's more about Santa than it is about Jesus. You can cry that that's a shame and it shouldn't be that way, but that would solely be your opinion. If you want it to be about Jesus then *you make your own* Christmas all about Jesus. But don't expect everyone else to, because it could very well mean something different to them. As I said, it wasn't about Jesus to begin with, so trying to make it all about the son of God under the guise of bring it "back to where it began" is a fallaciously motivated idea. So when you hear people saying Happy Holidays and see people writing Merry Xmas, don't bother saying it's a symptom of the holiday getting away from Jesus, because that makes little sense. It wasn't about him to begin with.

And while we're on the subject, when I was a kid I was told it was really bad to write "Xmas". "Keep (the word) Christ in Christmas." Nonsense. Xmas is just way easier. And it takes nothing away from the awesomeness of Jesus to write Xmas. I know that according to the Bible God is pretty particular about meaningless things, but come on, he's really going to get angry about a letter? I mean, how petty is your God? So it's perfectly proper for pedophile-protecting people like Pope John Paul II to be bestowed the stately status of sainthood, and that's fine with everyone, but typing X instead of Christ is just too much to ignore? Besides, if you did your research you'd find that the origin of that offensive X is actually the church! See, X comes from the Greek letter *Chi*, which is the first letter in the Greek word for *Christ*. So really, Christians were the first people that started to use X in that manner, and do you know why? For the same reason we do! It's easier! There's just no sensible reason, whether you're a believer or not, to be upset about "Xmas".

So What Would Jesus Do about this Merry Christmas vs. Happy Holidays issue? He'd probably tell you to focus your energies on more pressing matters, such as helping those in need and such. I know I shouldn't speak for Jesus, or God, for that matter. But I will say this. If your God really does get upset over trivialities such as someone writing the letter X or saying Happy Holidays, all while accepting repentance from thieves, child molesters, and murderers, well, again, you've got a jerk for a God whose got some fucked up priorities. He should get them straightened out. And so should you, so you can stop worrying about who says Happy Holidays and who says Merry Christmas and just enjoy the celebration. And for the love of your God, stop trying to control language. Focus your energy on the important things; the things that matter most. Like getting to the store before they run out of iPhones.

<u>**Happiness Awaits**</u>

A young woman suffers from mental illness for most of her life. She goes through many hardships and misfortunes. She commits suicide at the age of 28. Under her online obituary more than one person assures the family that she is "now in the loving arms of God". Another young woman who is also suffering from mental illness and has contemplated suicide sees the obituary and decides that enough is enough. She writes a note that says she also wants to be happy in heaven. She takes her own life.

A little girl's daddy suddenly dies of a massive heart attack. She is 12 years old. She is told her daddy is happy in heaven and she will one day see him again. She hangs herself in her bedroom. Her mom finds a noted that reads, "Dear Mum, please don't be sad, I just miss daddy so much, I want to see him again."

One of these stories is a hypothetical situation I invented. The other is a true story I read in the Daily Mail UK.

Heaven for Hitler

A sign outside Rose City Park United Methodist Church reads "God prefers kind atheists over hateful Christians – Tom Tate, Pastor".

Sorry Tom, but this isn't true, although it does sound nice. If you are familiar with your Bible you should know that God doesn't much care about kindness. He much prefers obedience. A rapist can get into heaven, as long as he repents before death. Same goes for a child-killer, mass murderer, or dance-song writer. No matter how horrible your actions in life are, you can always make up for it by declaring your belief in and obedience to God. He will forgive you if you truly repent. Forgiveness is one of the main themes of the Christian faith, remember? And they say atheists have no morals. Christianity lets you commit any and all atrocities and still worm your way into heaven; a place of everlasting bliss and happiness. "The sun sets on the just and the unjust alike."

Yes, Pastor Tom, whether you like to admit it or not, Adolf Hitler could be enjoying heaven right now, all according to *your* religion.

Help Wanted:
Applicant Must Be Recently Dead

One of the most infuriating things people say is "God needed another angel". I swear, if someone says that to me after I lose someone close to me I'm gonna demand they explain it to me. Then I might kick them in the chest. It seems to be most often said after the death of a child. Again, if someone said it to me after my child died? Forget about it.

For instance, I just read an article about a 47 year old grandmother who killed her two grandsons, 1 and 2 years of age, with a shotgun, before turning the gun on herself, and some fuckin' dimwit had actually written under the article, "God has two beautiful angels helping him now."

Helping him with *what?!* Why would God need these two angels? Why would God need any angel? He's God! Isn't he all-powerful and all-knowing? You're telling me he needs *help* with shit? Like what—putting up his Christmas lights? Are there jars he can't open? Does he need someone to bring him his beer? He needs an assistant, really? Who is he, Beyoncé? And he needs help from children? *Babies?!* How are babies going to help God? Please, tell me why God would need a baby angel.

Here's an idea for our loving, all-powerful Lord. If he needs some kind of baby-assistant to help him with whatever weird shit he's got on the go up there, how about he just create one for himself, rather than killing and taking them from down here?

Brent MacLean

<u>Hell Schmell</u>

Whenever I happen to have a conversation about beliefs with a religious moderate I inevitably discover that their beliefs aren't all that different from my own. I swear, every time, if the discussion lasts more than a few minutes, they eventually admit that they don't really know what the deal is when it comes to God either, which is all I've ever said. (Actually, most religious moderates seem to get angry after a few minutes of 'God talk'. I think this is because they know that they are getting dangerously close to agreeing with an evil atheist like me.)

What I've always wondered is if you aren't sure about God, Jesus, and all that, and you go along with the traditions like weddings and baptisms and such, doesn't that actually cheapen the ceremonies? It's funny because even though I'm a non-believer I respect the ceremonies enough to not partake in them and pretend to think them legitimate. Meanwhile, you're up there at the front of the church and the congregation (and God, don't forget him) and you're passing yourself off as a true believer, yet you really aren't sure. That's lying. In Church. To God. Not sure if you know this but according to the Bible you're on your way to hell. You cannot doubt God. You cannot question him. And you certainly can't lie to him.

But that knowledge doesn't bother you, of course, and I know why it doesn't. It's because you're not afraid of hell. And why aren't you afraid of hell? Because you're no more of a believer than I am.

Hold On To Your Hats!

I have no patience for the 'controversial' stories about women being made to remove their veils for certain situations like contract signing or court proceedings, or men that aren't allowed to wear turbans while doing police work. My thought is this: *Grow up!*

If your God is going to condemn you to an eternity of hell because you took a cloth garment off your head then may I be the first to suggest that your God is a fool, a prick, and not worth worshipping in the first place? God really cares about hats? Really? *Hats?*

So you're saying you can live your whole life as a good person, doing right by your family and all the people you come into contact with, and live as an honest person with integrity, yet at the gates of heaven God's gonna say, "Sure, you were about as good as a human can get..... but you took your hat off a couple times. Sorry. Rules are rules. Down you go. Okay, see you late—What's that? Oh, no, no. You will definitely not need a jacket down there. Right. Okay. See ya."

How I Know You Don't Believe

Here's how I know you don't truly believe in God.

The answer to the God Question is probably the most important thing we can know, individually. Whether or not there is a God that wants us to do and believe certain things matters to every single person on earth. It affects us all. Why? Because of the consequences. Or more specifically, the punishment. Seriously, if God exists, and he has rules he wants you to follow, wouldn't you say it would be pretty important for you to learn them? (Let's skip for now the part where we figure out which God is the real one.) Because what happens if you don't follow his rules? You burn in hell for eternity. Eternity! Wouldn't that possibility be a pretty good motivator for you to try to at least find out what you can do to, I dunno, avoid the eternal torture and suffering? I've heard many believers say, "I believe that if you're a good person you'll go to heaven." Well, where did you get that idea? You made it up! You can't make up the criteria for getting into heaven. If God exists like you say he does, then you're ignoring his rules and making up your own! That makes no sense and it's about as arrogant as one can get—deciding that you know better than God what constitutes a heaven-worthy person.

The point I'm trying to make is this. If you actually believed there is a God you would actually concern yourself with him, and most people hardly do at all. First, you'd want to make sure he existed. You'd read the arguments for and against his existence. We're talking about your eternal soul here; wouldn't you agree that's kind of important? Is it not worth it to read a book or two if it could mean saving your soul? Is a little investigation really too much to expect? Apparently it is indeed too much to expect.

Say you're an airplane pilot (what politically correct numbskulls might call a 'captain') and a stewardess (what politically correct numbskulls might call a 'flight attendant') comes into the cockpit (what politically correct numbskulls might call a 'flight deck') and tells you that there is a passenger on the plane who claims he has a bomb. She (let's remain politically incorrect and assume it's a woman) tells you this man says he'll blow up the plane killing everyone on board if you don't give in to his demands. But he also says that if you do everything he asks, you and the crew and the passengers will not be harmed, and you'll all get to go home to your loved ones very soon. Now wouldn't you say that whether or not this man exists is pretty important? Should you just say, "Well, I'm not sure if that man is really back there or not, so I'm just going to fly this plane as best I can. I'm sure that'll be good enough for him."? Of course not. Your life and the lives of everyone else on the plane are in jeopardy. The first thing you would do is use simple logic. You are as sure as you can be that this stewardess is completely serious about this man and his claim of having a bomb. She's not insane and she wouldn't be joking because such a joke would cause all sorts of problems for her, and everyone else. She has nothing to gain from such a fabrication. So you decide that there is definitely a man sitting back there that says that he has a bomb. What's next? You'll want to find out what his demands are, his commandments, if you will; what he wants you to do. You cannot be of the mindset I mentioned earlier and say, "I think that if I remain a good person and fly this plane well the hijacker will let us all go free." You would not make up your own criteria for keeping safe in a situation where the outcome is controlled by someone else, someone with the means to do you serious harm. You need to know his rules. So you would do just that: you would find out what the man wants of you. The same goes for God and his rules. He holds the fate of your eternal soul just as the hijacker holds the fate of your living being.

As I said, you'd first want to be sure God exists, rather than just assuming one does. But surely you'd also want to be sure *which* God exists, rather than simply picking the most convenient God to follow, which would most likely be the one your parents believed in. Because if you jump to the conclusion that one exists, and you simply decide without question that it's the Christian God for instance, then you could easily be mistaken, thus pissing off whatever God is actually running the show and making all the rules; rules that are different than the rules of the fake Christian God you chose to worship. The rules come from the one holding the power. Fate. Your fate. Ignoring this aspect would be like getting up from your pilot's seat, walking back to the passengers, kneeling down in front of the first man you come to, and saying, "Tell me what it is you want." Meanwhile the man with the bomb sits eight rows back, getting more fidgety by the minute. It's very important to figure out which passenger/God is the correct one; the one that is holding your life/eternal soul in his hands.

So you figure out which man is the hijacker. You ask the stewardess. She points him out. You talk to him and figure out pretty quick the guy is as serious as a bowl of coleslaw. He is legit. The same should go for your potential God. You need to find out which one is legit. It's important. And you do this by research and logic, such as reading all the arguments for and against the existence of God, or, in the plane scenario, doing what I described above. You find out if one exists and you find out which one it is.

Okay, so I've written out this weird analogy which may or may not make sense to you, and you're probably asking yourself, "But why did you say that you know that I don't believe?" The reason is this: You're not all that concerned about your eternal soul. You're not concerned all that much about whether or not God exists. You haven't asked countless questions. You haven't done the research. You haven't read any of the holy books. You also haven't read the books arguing for God existence. Nor have you read the books claiming that there's no evidence that God exists. Am I correct in these assumptions? There's a pretty good chance I am. See, if you were concerned you would have thought about it more. You would have done the research. But you're not concerned about it because deep down you know it's all nonsense. You know all these pastor/priest "experts" don't really know anything about the nature of reality. And even if you're one of the people that believes that our universe must have had a creator, and you consider yourself a believer in that manner, well, that simply means that you don't believe in God, Jesus, Allah, the Bible, the Qur'an, or any other *specific* religion, god, or holy text that exists on earth. You don't believe anyone knows anything about this creator—you just believe in some unknown creative entity. And that's fine. Just be honest with yourself about it. And keep in mind that with this sort of belief there are no rules to follow, unless you make up your own, and there's no heaven or hell, no punishment or reward, unless you make them up yourself.

But let's say you did somehow manage to settle on a particular God. Did you make any attempt to find out what his rules are or did you just shrug and say, "Eh. No one knows."? Because remember, if you don't follow those rules he might very well crash you into the lake of fire, or someplace equally unpleasant. I gotta say, I'd wanna know those rules. Have you ever had a hangnail? A bad sunburn? What about a migraine? Well, those are nothin' compared to what awaits you should you end up in hell. And not only is it excruciating pain, it's forever! Seems to me like that would be pretty important. Especially if there are ways to avoid it.

And then there's death. Wouldn't people that truly believed in this loving God who wants us to go to heaven rarely cry over death? They only would do so when they thought God wasn't opening the Pearly Gates for their particular dearly departed. If I knew my loved one was about to die and go to heaven to live in eternal bliss, how could I be anything but happy for him? I'd want him to stay here on earth with its pain and suffering and war and destruction when he could be living it up in paradise? No way man, I'd want him to be where it is best. I might miss him, but it would be selfish of me to wish him to stay here rather than move on to a place of eternal happiness. And many say they will "see them again" in heaven, assuming people get to reunite in heaven. Well if that's the case, there's even less reason to be upset when a loved one dies, again, unless you think you or your loved one is hell-bound. But don't misunderstand. I'm not saying there aren't people that are happy about loved ones dying. They exist. They really do. Oh, they're usually drowning their children or locking their families in a burning house to fast-track them to heaven, but they are out there. And that's the point. The few that are true believers are insane. You know it and I know it. They are crazy people and terrorists. Those are the only ones that are elated when people pass away. Rather than crying their balls off when their sister dies they are ecstatic. They are *happy*. But how often do you think regular, average Christians feel this way when they or someone they love is dying? It's pretty freakin' rare, I can guarantee you that. And it's because they aren't confident in their beliefs. They don't really believe it as fact. They aren't true believers. But those terrorists? Those guys were true believers. No one is going to blow themselves up willy-nilly just on a hunch that there's a God that's waiting to reward them when they do the deed. They're not just hoping that their beliefs are true, they are certain of it. So certain they devote their lives—and their deaths—to the cause of pleasing that God. That's true belief, and 99% of you Christians don't even come close to belief that strong. And that's a good thing. It's a discrepancy most people don't think about but there's a huge difference between actually believing something and just wanting to believe it. And if you're a reader of mine you probably already know that I posit that belief is not a choice. You do not choose what to believe. You can only choose what you *want* to believe and what decrees you want to follow. Actual belief is an involuntary and automatic action of a rational mind. (Please recall my 2+2=5 discussion from a previous post.)

So what does it all mean? It means that you care less about God than I do. See, I cared about God. I cared a lot. As a kid I just assumed what people told me about God was true. I assumed he was real, because I never thought adults would lie about such a thing. And since I believed there was a being with the ability to "crash my airplane" I wanted to know all about him; about what he wanted. You never gave it much thought because you never really believed there was a hijacker in the first place. It was as if the stewardess came to you and said, "Excuse me, Captain, but there's a fluorescent yellow alligator in row D and he says he wants you to know he holds the key to your salvation." You'd immediately pay it no mind because you'd know the stewardess is kidding, lying, or batshit crazy. Either way you're not going through the trouble of getting out of your seat to investigate this talking reptile. Nor are you spending your limited time on earth investigating the existence of any God, because you know deep down that the people that say they know God exists are either kidding, lying, or batshit crazy.

You might hope. You might want. But you don't *believe*. You're not gonna alter your life-course due to the far-fetched claims of a few. Nor are you altering your flight plan based on the far-fetched claims of a wacky flight attendant. You're not afraid of the yellow alligator. You know he doesn't exist. I know this because if you thought there was a chance he did and he held your life in his hands (claws?) you would get up and do something about it. But you don't. You just say, "I'll be good and things will be fine." That's a pretty confident assumption when it concerns your afterlife in blissful heaven versus your eternal suffering in hell. But you're not worried. You're concerned with the here and now. Because you know as well as I do that there's no reason to believe there is a God or a yellow alligator, because this is the real world and this life, this flight, is all we have.

Hugging Brian Greene

Often the Richard Dawkins Foundation will post questions they receive on their Facebook page. This was a recent one:

Do atheists have an issue with research on dead bodies or, more importantly, body farms?

Again and again (and again!) I encounter people that don't know what atheism or being an atheist means. I guess it shouldn't surprise me since having a religious affiliation is so ingrained in our collective conscious that people often automatically think everyone belongs to some sort of group, and subscribes to some pre-written document or idea. This misconception bothers me only when I hear it from people that claim they read this blog. I say, "You don't seem to understand what 'atheist' means."

"Yes I do."

"I thought you said you read my blog?"

"I do, all the time."

"You mustn't, because I explain over and over what atheist means."

You can ask 1000 atheists that question about dead bodies and body farms and get 1000 different answers. There are no rules, no doctrine, nothing to follow. In fact, it's possible that the only thing these 1000 people have in common is that when asked, "Do you believe in God?" the answer will be "No". That's it. That's all it means. A-theist: not a theist (how many times have I written that?) I once had a (particularly crazy) Christian lady say something about how I don't believe anything happens after we die. I asked her why she assumed that I thought nothing happened after we die, since I never mentioned it. She said, "Well, you're an atheist. Isn't that what atheists believe? Shouldn't you know what your group believes?" That really is a misguided and ignorant thing to say. I tried to explain to her that I don't belong to a group per se. I can be categorized with others that don't see any evidence for God, sure, but beyond that I may or not agree with anything another atheist may or may not believe. Surely, many atheists are more scientific-minded and tend to ask questions and wait for evidence before subscribing to a belief, but that just goes with the territory. But does that make us a 'group', just because we know that empirical evidence is a necessary precursor to knowledge? That notion should apply to every human being in the world, no?

I really don't like going over this stuff again and again. (Really. I don't.) But it seems that this misunderstanding keeps popping up, and not just among the religious. People I know, people that are asking the God Question, seem to get stuck on this one point; and it's a major point. *Atheism is not a religion.* We're not the opposite side of the religious coin. We're not on the coin at all. I'm sure most of us realized we were atheists because we saw fit to ask questions concerning God. See, it's all about questions. Sometimes we get answers. Sometimes we don't get answers. And if we don't, we don't use blind faith to make up our own. You can take any of the old analogies:

"Atheism is a religion like OFF is a television channel."

"Atheism is a religion like bald is a hair colour."

"Atheism is a religion like not collecting stamps is a hobby."

They all apply.

On an episode of the amazing *Fabric of the Cosmos* series (which I highly recommend) physicist and string theorist Brian Greene was talking about the Multiverse Theory. That's the theory that our universe is just one of an infinite amount of universes that simultaneously exist with ours. Some scientists feel that this theory is valid, although we may never be able to prove it. Greene said, "So should we *believe* in the Multiverse Theory? Well, no, because we can't believe in anything without evidence, but...." and I swear, I could have climbed through the television and hugged him.

And that's what being an atheist is about, for me. Not hugging Brian Greene, but that we don't believe in any Gods because there hasn't been any evidence presented to prove that any exist. I think most that subscribe to this idea will apply it to other things as well. In fact, most believers themselves subscribe to this empirical evidence idea in their day-to-day lives, but they suspend it when it comes to God. But that just makes no sense. Why reject your own rationale for one topic only?

I Now Baptize You...
Progressive Conservative

If you're so willing to decide for your child what their religious beliefs are, and you go through the trouble of having a magical ceremony to officially label them a Christian before they can even say "da da", why don't you also enroll them in a particular political party that you fancy? Why not make them a Liberal or a Conservative, or a Democrat or a Republican? If you're so eager to label your child, rather than letting them grow up, learn, weigh their options, and *decide for themselves* what organizations they may or may not want to join, why not decide as well if they are communist, socialist, or democratic while you're at it? Telling someone your baby is a Christian makes just as much sense as saying your baby is a Marxist.

I want to ask parents, "What's so bad about *not* getting your baby Christened? What will happen if you don't? Why not let the poor child decide for herself when she's old enough to understand what it's all about?" Of course, it's not kosher to ask such questions, so I have to refrain from doing so. Although I have noticed it's perfectly fine to ask someone why they *aren't* getting their baby baptized. Isn't that incredible? But it's pretty indicative of how religion has turned everything backwards. You pour magic water over your baby's head for reasons 99% of people do not know, but I cannot ask you why you did it. But if I *don't* pour magic water over my baby's head, well then, that's just crazy! "How come you didn't pour magic water over your baby?!" And people wonder why I say I'm living in a perpetual *Twilight Zone,* where I'm the only sane one among a world of insane people, which of course makes me the weird one; the insane one.

I must say, it's not lost on me that no one has ever said,

72

"We Christened our baby so it wouldn't go to hell." Because, as I'm sure some of you know, many denominations adhere to the doctrine of Original Sin. The gist of this idea is that because of Adam and Eve's disobedience in the Garden of Eden, God made it so every person henceforth was born infused with sin. In other words, every person ever born was born a sinner, without ever actually sinning. Think of it as a virus or defective gene that's passed from parent to baby that started with those two rascals who couldn't keep their hands off God's precious fruit. Because of this Original Sin, a baby is a sinner until the moment the Christening or baptism washes away that sin, and opens up the "flow of grace" from God to the baby's heart. Then, in the unfortunate event the baby should die, it will go straight to heaven. Of course, you might have already guessed what happens if the infant passes away before it is baptized. It goes to hell. Yup, that's what the doctrine says. The baby could be 4 seconds old—doesn't matter. It's already a sinner, and without God's grace washing away that sin, it will burn in hell for eternity. (Many denominations have lightened up on this aspect of Original Sin, some by saying the baby will actually end up in Limbo for eternity, not hell.) To add insult to horrific injury, these unbaptized babies were for much of the past, looked upon with something akin to disgust. They were considered unclean. So much so, in fact, that many cemeteries forbade unbaptized babies from being buried in the regular, sacred ground, with everyone else. Sometimes they were allowed near the main cemetery, but were banished to their own "special" section. The largest cemetery serving my hometown has such a section. Down over a little hill, completely segregated from the other 15,000 plots, are a small collection of tiny graves.

What bothers me most about this whole baptism thing—besides the early start on the brainwashing to come—is that it's one of those lingering superstitious traditions that religious moderates, and even non-believers, still cling to. Christenings, weddings, funerals, Easter, Christmas, and Good Friday are all events that the 'barely religious' keep alive. I just don't get it. But as I stated above, they often get irritated by folks like me that have the gall to question it, so I rarely get to. Most of these people are normal, rational folks, but they simply will not let go of these outdated (and just plain silly) ceremonies. I believe religious moderates are a bigger problem in our society than religious fundamentalists. I really do. See, the moderates know better. Deep down they do. The fundamentalists do not. They're just too far out of it. The moderates do not even attempt to live their lives according to the Scriptures. They are free people; free people that, for some reason, give superstitious beliefs and traditions far too much respect. The problem of course is that if you give unfounded beliefs complete and total respect then you automatically give the fundamentalists—and religious terrorists— the very same courtesy, because you cannot say that one unlikely belief is any more valid than another. The technicalities of what people believe are actually irrelevant. Believing that Jesus walked on water is just as ridiculous as believing that 72 virgins await the suicide bomber in heaven. One can lead to more actual devastation, but it's no more unlikely.

It would be nice if Western culture chose to leave children out of it. In every other aspect of child rearing we're sensitive to individuality and refrain from forcing our own hopes and dreams upon our children. Parents that try to "live through their kids" are looked down upon. We encourage distinctiveness and unique life endeavors when it comes to our children's minds, personalities, and careers. Only when it comes to religion are we so willing to funnel them into a previously-decided confine. Only with religion do we happily stunt their intellectual growth and suppress their thoughts and minds. Just today I saw a study that said that children raised with religion have a much harder time distinguishing between fact and fiction, when compared to children raised without the fog of religion clouding their judgment of what is real and what is not. Only with religion do we do our best to give them our worst, and we start as soon as possible with labels such as Anglican and Catholic and Baptist. It's fine if they grow up and research churches (or political parties, or governmental affiliations) on their own and decide that they want to join. That's called free will and freedom of choice, and it's a wonderful thing. So why would you want to take that away from your own children? To attach a label to your child before they can grasp the concept of it, a concept 99% of adults find nearly impossible to comprehend themselves, is to do your child and early and dreadful disservice.

I Swear on My Mother's Life
This is the Best Post You Will Ever Read

I think it's amusing how seriously people take "swearing on the life" of someone.

I watched one season of *Survivor* many years ago (I had only one channel at the time) and during the game a woman swore on the life of her children that she hadn't formed an alliance with so and so. Turns out she lied. During the final show some other contestants ridiculed her for it. I don't mean they voiced their displeasure—I mean they insulted her, vilified her, and did their best to make her feel like she was an immoral person, and even a horrible mother. And it seemed like she actually started to feel bad about it. What bullshit. It's meaningless. If I say, "I swear on the life of my mother that I can bench 375lbs" do you actually think it will have any negative effect on my mom? Do you really think something bad will happen to me as a result? Get real and start thinking like a mature adult, will ya? What's next? Are adults going to start validating contractual agreements with pinky swears? "Your Honour, it was a binding contract! *He pinky swore on it!*"

It's a stupid superstition and that *Survivor* woman should have been commended for using a childish notion of bad luck against people dumb enough to take it seriously.

If Christ Wasn't Busy Painting His Shed His Power Would Compel You!

In every one of these 'possession' movies like *The Exorcist, The Possession*, and *The Exorcism of Emily Rose*, the families of the demon-infused kiddies always call in priests to help—with the aid of God—oust the intruding impish interloper. Although one might assume God actually knows about the possession long before mommy and daddy even notice a change in little Suzy's behavior, given his all-knowingness. One might even think God knew it would happen beforehand, what with his Divine Plan and all, but let's leave that out for now.

My question is this: Why wouldn't God just kick the demon out from the get-go? Why do the priests have to waste time chanting and throwing magic water about? If God agrees that the demonic possession isn't cool and wants to get rid of it, why does he wait until he's coaxed to get involved? Is he that friggin' lazy? "Okay, I heard you a hundred times: 'The power of Christ compels you'—I know! Jesus, fine, I'll help. Hang on. Where's my jacket?"

And why is there always such a struggle? Isn't God supposed to be super strong? I thought he was all-powerful. That's what most people seem to think. I suppose it's possible he's more like Jon Jones. Pretty much unbeatable, but every now and then a Daniel Cormier comes along and gives him a run for his money.

Brent MacLean

<u>Ignorant by Choice</u>

Here's a valuable tip for all you atheists out there that enjoy discussing religion with believers. At the very beginning of the conversation ask them this question:

If there were no God would you even want to know?

If they don't immediately say yes you'd be wise to save your breath.

<u>The Insufferable Saved</u>

Think about all the hardcore Christians out there. I'm sure you've come across at least a few in your life. Think about those people, the ones that cannot wait for Jesus to return to cast away the evil folk (like me) and take them, the true believers, back to heaven with him to live for all eternity. Think about those people; what they're like, what they say and do. Think about their personalities, character, and beliefs—religious, political, and moral. Think of the music and the entertainment they like. Think of the news they watch. Think of what they deem important in life. Think of what they think of us; what they think of themselves. Think of how they think the world should be.

Now that you've thought about all this, ask yourself this: Would Jesus really want to spend an eternity with these people? Would you?

Brent MacLean

It's a St. Patrick's Day Miracle!

I've noticed that any time something really good happens around Christmastime people call it a "Christmas miracle", but whenever anything really good happens any other time of the year it's just a... miracle. There are no Valentine's Day miracles. I've never heard of a 4th of July miracle. No one talks about any Orangemen's Day miracles. I've never even heard of an Easter miracle. Only during Christmas does the time of year get attached to the miracle. Why is that?

I think it's because people are silly and long for fairy tales to be true. It makes the miracle more magical, and people love magic. If Jimmy gets a new lung on December 22nd then it's a Christmas miracle straight from God because it's Christmas and God is extra generous around his son's birthday. But when are the Christmas miracle cutoffs? If Barbara wakes up from a 17-year coma on November 29th is that close enough to the holiday season to call it a Christmas miracle, or is it just a normal miracle? Is that even Christmastime? Some people have their Christmas trees up by then. Does that count? If little Sammy becomes cancer-free on January 7th does that count as a Christmas miracle? I have no idea.

Jesus Probably Tapped...
A Lot

['Tapping out' is essentially giving up in an MMA match. It could be the result of a submission hold, a barrage of strikes, or because the fighter suffered a bone broken. It's essentially how a fighter quits.]

Jesus Didn't Tap is a popular phrase among many MMA fighters. The slogan is on shirts, shorts and jackets. Many guys even have the phrase tattooed on their bodies. I assume they're using Jesus as a source of strength and inspiration, but, as you might have guessed, I think it's stupid.

Let's say the whole Jesus story actually happened (when we all know it very likely didn't). Where does it say that he didn't tap, that he didn't say, "Hey! Knock it off, will ya!"? Also, even if he did tap what good would it have done? Do you think that these guys that were ordered to torture a man that claimed to be the King of the Jews would have stopped if they noticed he was tapping his hand on the ground? What a stupid idea. "Hey, Albanus! He's tapping out. Yup. He tapped. Let's let him go. It's the rules."

But let me get a little more philosophical. Jesus, who is also God, set this whole thing in motion, because he, God, who is also Jesus, had a Divine Plan that involved Jesus, who is also God, getting betrayed, tortured, and killed, so that he, Jesus, who is also God, could die "for our sins" so that we may "be forgiven" for betraying, torturing, and killing Jesus, who is also God, *by* God, who is also Jesus, so that we may live forever and "be with" God, who is also Jesus.

So saying Jesus Didn't Tap is useless. Of course he didn't. Because even if tapping out was an option he wouldn't have done so because he knew full well that what was occurring was all a part if his own Divine Plan and it's the way things were *supposed* to happen. Tapping out would have messed up his entire plan and the *execution* of that plan up to that point. It would just have wasted his own precious time, and God isn't about to go wasting time. He's very punctual. It's what I like most about him.

<u>The Land of Facts</u>

At this point, debating the fact of evolution is akin to arguing whether or not the earth is round.

Eventually, when something has so much evidence for it, it becomes a fact, and if you want to disprove that fact, you have to present some pretty powerful evidence to negate the mountain of evidence supporting it. This certainly applies to evolution, which magician and skeptic James Randi calls "the single, unifying scientific explanation for the diversity of life on Earth, and the foundation upon which the biological sciences are built."

If you happen to be someone that denies the fact of evolution, a person biologist Richard Dawkins would call a "history-denier", I'm willing to bet that you simply haven't read up on it, and there's a good chance you don't actually understand it. The amount of evidence for evolution is beyond staggering. The number of scientists that support evolution is staggering. Yet, I come across regular everyday people all the time that simply shrug it off. I wanna shake them. First, because I know they haven't even attempted to learn about the very thing they are denying. Second, because they are laypeople! And I always cringe when Average Joe's simply ignore the empirical findings of the world's most brilliant minds. And that's exactly what is happening with this resistance to the theory of evolution. If the world's physicists suddenly started saying they have found, through testing and evidence, that black holes actually connect our universe to a neighbouring universe, I would say, "Huh. That's crazy." I might even say, "That's hard for me to wrap my head around." And then, if I'm interested, I would *read about* this new discovery, as wacky as it might sound to me. Notice what I did *not* do? I did not say they were wrong just because I didn't think the idea made much sense. I didn't presume that I knew better than expert scientists and their findings. But that's what millions of people do every day when it comes to evolution.

Am I saying that whatever a scientist says is automatically fact? Absolutely not. As I have written elsewhere, the brilliance of modern science lies in part due the competitive nature of the scientists themselves. They want to be the ones to find out new things, to be responsible for exciting breakthroughs. Does that mean ego is involved? Absolutely! But it's in a good way! If Dr. Jones discovers an amazing new fact, is he going to receive respect, admiration, and possibly some fame? Quite likely, but not before this new discovery has been *verified*. See, every other scientist don't just adopt this new fact. They want to verify it. Everyone wants to be sure; everyone wants to *know*. Everything is *peer reviewed*, and that is the key difference between science and faith.

When a scientist or a laboratory discovers something new, they first test and retest it themselves. Since their findings will be critiqued by their peers they want to be sure about whatever it is they're proposing. The proponents of this would-be fact compile enough evidence to be confident their conclusions are correct, and *then* it's presented to the scientific world (which sometimes includes competing scientists and labs) to be critiqued, questioned, and re-analyzed. It's a wonderful way of weeding out the nonsense. Facts aren't made up willy-nilly. And even if they were they'd quickly be quashed by the rest of the intellectual world. Religion operates in the opposite manner. Someone says something, anything, no matter how unlikely or improbable, and under the protection we have bestowed upon religious belief, no one is able to question or criticize it at all. How convenient for the religious! They have free reign to create "facts" and no one is allowed to question them! The difference between these two approaches is summed up nicely in a Facebook Share graphic I once saw that read "Science: Because figuring things out is better than making shit up."

What's most depressing about this is that the average person, the religious moderate, and even many non-believers, so often give more weight to the claims of the religious over the empirical evidence compiled by the scientists. It's utterly maddening. *Here, I have run tests again and again and each time the results are conclusive. And also, scientists all over the world have evaluated my methods and findings and have even run their own tests, and all agree that my findings are correct.* "No, thanks. I'm going to ignore what you have found through empirical data and go with what people that lived thousands of years ago, long before modern science, had to say about the nature of the universe, even though they offer no evidence, much less any proof." Sounds silly when you see it written out, right? Look, if you're not interested in this stuff then just leave it alone. There's nothing wrong with saying, "I don't know." That's fine and surely a hell of a lot better than arguing against something you know and care nothing about. It's certainly better than saying, "No, I think the priests have this all figured out," because, let's be honest, if you're ignoring the educated experts on this subject, it's perfectly reasonable to assume you will ignore educated experts from other fields, instead choosing to believe the groundless claims by the religious. So instead of going to your doctor for medical advice, why don't you go to a minister? Instead of going to an accountant, see what a priest has to say about how you should invest your hard earned money. When your car's engine starts to squeal and smoke, be sure to locate your nearest pastor. Stupid ideas, right? Well, so is trusting these people when it comes to cosmology, astronomy, physics, and biology!

And besides the fact the people are ignoring this strikingly uneven *peer-reviewed evidence vs. no evidence needed* conflict, they aren't even paying attention to the very basic elements of the theory of evolution; the basic idea. Nowhere is this ignorance more evident than in the sentiment that "I diddin come from no monkey!"

Nobody is claiming "we came from monkeys". Got that? I will type it again in slightly different words: We humans did not evolve from monkeys and no one says we did. Humans share a *common ancestor* with the apes that exist today, and if you go further back, with monkeys. I've actually heard people, real live adult humans, say, "When a monkey gives birth to a human I'll believe in evolution." As unbelievable a statement as that is, it's a bit hard not to feel sorry for such folks. These people actually believe that scientists are claiming that one species of animal sometimes gives birth to a whole new species of animal. Do I need to explain why that's the dumbest thing any human has ever said other than, "Kings of Leon are the best band ever"? Well, I'm not going to explain it. That's not what this post was meant to be about. If you are interested in how evolution works there are countless resources. (The Richard Dawkins book *The Magic of Reality: How We Know What's Really True* is a wonderful book. I highly recommend it to anyone interested in science, even on the most basic level.) I will however say this: evolution has no goal; no purpose. There seems to be an idea that we humans are at the top of an evolutionary lineage. I'm sure you've seen the illustration of the little monkey that precedes a bigger primate, which precedes an upright ape, all the way to a fully upright human. This is not an accurate picture of evolution. Every animal on earth is as evolved as every other animal. All lines of life do not lead to us. If you can watch cows long enough they will not eventually evolve into us. This idea that we are the pinnacle of evolution stems from our own egos as well as the religious notion that we're special. We are not. We just happened to end up in the lucky spot—lucky for us, not so much for other animals—of having high intelligence. In the Judeo-Christian myth God gave

Adam and all his descendants dominion over the animals. But that's just a story. Contrary to what arrogant believers think, the world was not created for us.

Another misconception that I have to mention is this confusion about the word *theory*. Deniers love to shout "Evolution is just a theory!" as if it's some sort of knockout blow against what Dr. Dawkins calls "a fact. Beyond reasonable doubt, beyond serious doubt, beyond sane, informed, intelligent doubt, beyond doubt evolution is a fact. The evidence for evolution is at least as strong as the evidence for the Holocaust, even allowing for eye witnesses to the Holocaust. It is the plain truth..." And it's a plain pity that so many people don't seem to realize there is more than one meaning to the word theory. In scientific terms a theory can still be *a demonstrable fact*. When people say "evolution is just a theory", they are making it clear that they don't understand the meaning of the word. I bet they'd be surprised to learn that heliocentricism, the model that states that the earth and the other planets revolve around a stationary sun, is "just a theory" as well. That's right; it's called the *theory of heliocentricism*. But who would deny that we know *for a fact* that the earth revolves around the sun? Who would say, "Yeah, I know scientists *say* the earth orbits the sun, but I don't believe it because it's just a theory." If these fact-deniers were at all self-aware or consistent in their beliefs that is exactly what they'd say. For these people, the monumental evidence compiled that supports evolution by the world's intellectual elite doesn't suffice as convincing evidence. But a Bronze Age book written by unkown, unenlightened people long before we knew about bacteria, that claims that virgins had babies and men walked on water, is totally legitimate. It's hilarious and depressing.

Here are two *Oxford English Dictionary* definitions of the word *theory*:

#1 A scheme or system of ideas or statements held as an explanation or account of a group of facts or phenomena; a hypothesis that has been confirmed or established by observation or experiment, and is propounded or accepted as accounting for the known facts; a statement of what are held to be the general laws, principles, or causes of something known or observed.

#2 A hypothesis proposed as an explanation; hence, a mere hypothesis, speculation, conjecture; an idea or set ideas about something; an individual view notion.

While the second definition is indeed valid, it is just one of many. The "just a theory" people are either unaware that the first definition exists, or they knowingly ignore it because it doesn't suit their needs. Christians are quite adept at this sort of thing. Just look at how they assert the validity and importance of specific parts of the Old Testament, while dismissing the countless instances of pure insanity, because the New Testament supposedly makes some Old Testament stories invalid. But just *some*. Well, you don't get to make personal rules in that manner. If you do you're in the world of subjective opinions and far away from the land of objective facts.

I know they'd hate to hear it but when the word *theory* is used in the phrase the *theory of evolution*, it is invoking the first definition. It is a fact. It has been demonstrated over and over. It is "a hypothesis that has been confirmed or established by observation or experiment." As one biologist recently said, "No reputable scientist disputes it." Whether or not you *like* the idea of evolution, whether or not it fits into your religion's particular doctrine or creation myth, whether or not you understand it, evolution is a scientific fact. It's not a case of "do you believe in evolution?" anymore. We're far past that. It's now a case of "Do you choose to ignore the fact of evolution that has been clearly demonstrated through valid testing methods that have undergone peer evaluation in order to verify its validity, or do you simply choose to ignore it?"

The Lies in the Skies

Out of all the superstitions we have in our society, from broken mirror bad luck to God and Jesus, from birthday wishes to mutilating—uh, I mean *circumcising*—infant males, none is so utterly stupid, nonsensical, and downright laughable, as astrology. For an adult to read horoscopes with any expectation of validity is nothing short of astonishing.

Where do these little tidbits of information come from anyway? Who is deciding that today is the day you should make a financial investment? Who is the person that figured out that you will meet someone from your past today? Is some mystical dude sitting somewhere, looking at the stars, which are somehow telling him what a particular day will bring about for five hundred million people all around the world? There are only 12 astrological signs to choose from, right? So are you telling me that every Capricorn is going to have the same general experience that day? Are you serious? Does it traverse countries, age, and cultures? Is a person in Houston, Texas that was born on January 2nd going to have the same kind of day that a tribesman in sub-Saharan Africa will have because they were born on the same day?

What about twins? Their horoscopes are always identical. So how does that work? They both can't have the same shit going on the entire time can they?

People often call superstitious beliefs harmless. And for the most part I'm sure they are. But for some believers it's anything but. Believe it or not, there are people making life-decisions with astrology and similar nonsense as their guiding voice of reason. But that voice isn't real! It doesn't exist. So who are they really listening to? I recently saw a woman on TV that was actually relocating from the US to England because her astrological reading told her that employment abroad would be a good move. So you can see how these silly horoscopes that are "all in good fun" can harm people. There are actually people that base who they will and will not date on such things. That too can mess with someone's life. "What? He's a *Scorpio?!* Oh well, fuck him! Sure he seems nice, ambitious and successful and kind.... but our signs aren't compatible!" Some might think, "Well, if those people are too stupid to know the difference then who cares?" Okay, fine. I guess it comes down to whether or not you think people that take advantage of others, to the point that their lives may be ruined, should be stopped. So-called "psychics" prey on the weak and vulnerable all the time. Should we just say, "Who cares?" or should these crooks be stopped?

One friend who believes in this garbage once said to me, in attempt to convince me of its validity, "You don't believe in astrology? Man, this stuff is older than God." Do I really need to explain why that statement means nothing? Just because something predates God (I assume he meant the Christian God) it's automatically valid? Should we go back to the earliest known beliefs and religions and start abiding by them? If it's all about antiquity then I suppose we should.

The fact that astrology still exists is indeed pretty sad. It's no different than reading tea leaves, getting your fortune told by some freaky chick at a flea market, or asking a Magic 8 Ball questions. It's false. It's not real. I think that the people that make money off this stuff are nothing short of scum. As I stated above, some people put so much faith into this bullshit that they alter their lives according to bogus advice, while others end up in financial ruin from spending money on this nonsense. In a society of critical-thinkers like our own, you'd think such a thing would never happen. But it does.

And the Lord Sayeth, "This Seat is Taken."

On July 20th of 2012 in Aurora, Colorado a man opened fire in a movie theater that was premiering a new *Batman* movie. 12 people were killed, and over 58 were injured by gunfire. There was a movie-goer who was sitting with his wife and child in the seat closest to the side-door from which the shooter would eventually emerge. But before the movie began the man decided to move his family to the balcony. He and his family survived the tragedy. The people that sat in their vacated seats did not. And this moron actually had the balls to go on television and say that God was watching over him and his family.

So this means that God was *not* watching over the people that were killed. Those poor people that died, I guess God didn't see fit to save them; to get *them* to switch seats; to make their cars run out of gas on the way to the theater; to make the shooter's gun jam; to give the shooter an aneurysm that morning, so everyone could be saved. I mean, that's what this idiot survivor is saying: God saved *me* by getting *me* to choose safer seats, but he didn't do the same for others.

And how dare people thank God for Gabrielle Giffords' miraculous recovery after being shot while 9 year old Christina Taylor-Green and five other victims lie in their graves. As I've said 277,590 times before, if you thank God for controlling a situation that automatically means you believe he controlled the bad things that happened too. Cherry-picking his influence is ridiculous. And I know some people try the "God only does good stuff" line, but that's based on nothing other than the person's own opinion. Read your Bible. God does not only do good things. Nor does he not want us to do only good things. In fact, in the Good

Book, God does plenty of things most people would find morally reprehensible. And if you think God stepped in to save Ms. Giffords or Mr. Chosen Movie-Goer, yet had nothing to do with the deaths of the others, you're at least saying that he chose them to survive while letting others die. And if that's the case, he's not the kind of Supreme Being that deserves praise. It's like 'America's Best Christian' Betty Bowers said, "Thanking God for sparing you in a natural disaster is like sending a thank-you note to a serial killer for stabbing the family next door."

That's one of the most irritating things about religious moderates—when they thank God after a catastrophe or tragedy that takes the lives of others. They are so arrogant as to think God 'chose' them to live while letting those less fortunate, un-chosen, *and less special,* people die. I wonder what the family of those killed would think of that idea; how God selected a few special folks to make it out while their loved ones were shot and killed by some psycho nutcase. Actually, they'd probably say, "God needed another angel".

If you survived an incident in which other people have died be thankful. Be happy. Be grateful. But also be humble in knowing that it was just the luck of circumstance. There was no divine father figure singling you out as one of his favourite kids. It's a childish way of thinking and you should be ashamed and embarrassed by it. "I'm special, you're not. God likes me more. He saved me. He let you die." It's really the whole "Does God answer prayers?" question. The people that say he does answer prayers are claiming God can and do control things that happen to us lowly humans. The funny (or irritating) thing is, when it comes to the bad stuff, the same people never ask why God would do such a thing, or at least intervene to prevent the tragedy from occurring. Because, according to these people, he certainly has that ability. They say things like, "Well, humans caused that tragedy." They invoke free will. But they believe God can control us and our situations! They said God got Mr. Chosen Movie-Goer to move to safer seats. Well, what about *his* free will? God seems to have overridden it altogether. Why does God override the free will of a few normal people, but can't or won't do the same for the free will of the murderous loner? How about making him decide to change his evil plans? I cannot count how many times a Christian has invoked free will when trying to explain this situation to me. Human does a bad thing? Free will. Human does something that leads to him being saved from a tragedy? God influenced it. It's ridiculous and it explains nothing. And if you are one of these people that believes God sometimes helps out, then that automatically cancels the idea of free will. Free will isn't free if someone else has the ability to alter it.

Seth MacFarlane, the creator of *Family Guy* and *American Dad*, was supposed to be on one of the planes that crashed into the World Trade Center. He slept in. He missed his flight. Naturally every interviewer that discovers this bit of trivia pokes and prods him for those "I thank God, I am blessed, God saved me" answers. Well, Seth is a rational and intelligent guy. He shrugs and says, "I've slept in and missed many flights." He doesn't think he's special. He doesn't think he was chosen by God to survive while thousands of others perished. He sees it as what it was: a bunch of events that played out. Luckily for him, those events led to him missing the flight. Why must so many take lucky occurrences and attach some supernatural element to them? There's no need. It makes no sense to do so.

I'd really like to ask Mr. Chosen Movie Goer guy why God didn't see fit to save everyone else. I'm willing to bet I'd get a "God works in mysterious ways" answer. Well, as Jim Jefferies said, "There's nothing mysterious about being an asshole!" Because if your God was indeed protecting only a select few from the bullets spraying from the madman's gun, let me be the first to suggest that that's exactly what your God is.

The Loyal Betrayal

I was watching the episode of *An Idiot Abroad* where Karl Pilkington is in Mexico during Easter. They love Jesus down there. Freakin' love him. But they don't celebrate Easter the way we do. Apparently painting eggs and telling our children a bunny rabbit left chocolate for them while they slept makes a bit too much sense for those wacky Mexicans. Alright. Whatever.

In the scene that inspired this post the people were carrying around big paper-mache effigies of frogs and cows and other things that were loaded with fireworks. They would light the fireworks and run like hell as the dude carrying the exploding effigy chased them around. It looked extremely dangerous. Karl said it was "fuckin' mental". A local fellow told Karl that the effigies they burn and explode are meant to represent Judas Iscariot, the man that betrayed Jesus Christ. They hate Judas. In fact, in our own culture, the very name Judas represents the ultimate in treachery. He's the quintessential double-crosser. If someone calls you Judas (or a Judas) they are definitely not paying you a compliment; quite the opposite. (Every Bob Dylan fan knows about the infamous "Judas" incident.) Even if the Jesus story were true, which it probably isn't, I think it makes no sense to vilify poor Judas. Here's why.

The fact that Jesus was crucified and "died for our sins" (whatever that means), well, that's pretty much the main component of the faith. That's why Christians love him so much, because he went through all the whipping and beating and hair pulling for us. But without Judas none of that would have happened and the Jesus story would be much less exciting. And what would Christians use to try to guilt non-believers with if not for how much Jesus suffered "for us"?

Isn't it reasonable to assume Jesus (and God—remember, they are part of the same entity) *knew*, *wanted*, and *made* Judas do what he did. It was all part of the Divine Plan, because God controls all, no? Didn't he "give his only son" (which was himself, but let's not get bogged down in confusion at the moment) for us? Surely no one is suggesting God gave his son *not* knowing that he would be crucified. Surely they're not saying he sent his only son simply to do some carpenter work with sermons on the side. So isn't it safe to assume that God gave his son with the purpose that he be crucified? I mean, I keep hearing that he gave "his only son to die for our sins". And if there is a Divine Plan, which many Christians claim there is (when it suits their needs, that is), wouldn't it also be safe to assume Judas Iscariot was simply doing what he was supposed to—nay, had to do? What I'm saying is that everyone seems to agree that Jesus' crucifixion was super-cool for us, after all, he did it *for* us, to help us, although I'm still not sure why, and Judas helped the whole plan along. And correct me if I'm wrong, but didn't Jesus actually *tell* Judas that he, Judas, would eventually betray him? The bottom line is that whether or not you believe in the Divine Plan, Judas played an important and pivotal role in the events that would eventually be known as the "The Greatest Story Ever Told". If there was a plan, he had no choice, and if there were no plan, God could have stopped him from betraying Jesus in the first place! If betraying Jesus was such a bad thing, so much so that it makes Judas an unforgivable and evil man, why didn't God just not let it happen? He has the power to stop things. Every Christian believes that. If they did not they would never pray to him and ask for favours. God could have just kicked Judas in the nuts, temporarily rendering him immobile, so he couldn't go and rat Jesus out to the authorities. Or he could have simply changed Judas' mind. Or how about skipping the whole thing and having whatever the crucifixion was supposed to accomplish just happen without the betrayal, torture, and crucifixion? Why go through all the trouble if the idea was to help us?

Take this scenario for instance. Rather than saying, "I'm going to make one guy get beaten and tortured and killed and afterward everyone gets a Nintendo Switch," why not just skip the first part? Why bother with the harsh stuff if you have the ability to just give everyone a Switch? So that everyone learns a lesson? Fine, but if you find it necessary to make everyone go through a process, you can't be mad at the pawn for acting as your instrument in implementing that process. The logical (ha!) response to all this would be that things just played out as Jesus/God intended. It's the reason Jesus showed up at all, isn't it?

So, my dear Mexican friends, lay off Judas, will ya? If you're still that upset that Jesus suffered and died you should redirect your anger to the true culprit behind the crucifixion: God.

Magic for the Children

Christmas is such a crock.

I'm not even talking about the fake religious aspects of it, even though they are indeed annoying; especially when non-religious people pretend to care about God and Jesus for a few days. Seriously, if I was a church-goer and I saw the once-a-year dickheads strolling into church on Christmas Eve I'd be livid. "What, you think God only pays attention in late December?!" Plus there's the fact that Christmas, or at least the celebration, was around long before Christianity. It was a pagan ritual celebrating the winter solstice. When Christianity began to gain traction in the 4th century they incorporated it into their whole scene. But that's not important for this post. I can handle all that silly stuff, annoying as it can be. What I dislike most about Christmas is the twisted logic people heap upon its purpose. An atheism-hating relative of mine once said "Christmas is about family and giving." I responded, "Oh. I thought it was about celebrating the birth of your Lord and Saviour."

Besides the fact that my wife and I have made it no secret that we are not Christian (we had no religious elements whatsoever in our wedding ceremony and our child has not been and will not be Baptized) we still celebrate Christmas. Why? Well, as I answered that very same atheism-hating relative of mine, "We celebrate it for the same reasons you do: because everyone else does. We just go along." On further thought though, I realized that's not entirely accurate. I wouldn't have celebrated it at all (before I had a child) if I was alone. But my wife has always enjoyed it. She would and will always celebrate Christmas, with or without me. She likes the decorations, the tree, the lights, the food, and the family get-togethers. Plus now we both like having

Christmas for our daughter. I have tried in past (pre-daughter) years to omit myself from it all, but it is damn near impossible. People will force it upon you. Seriously, if you tell your relatives to not get you anything because you are no longer celebrating Christmas they will look at you as if you said you had decided to become a serial rapist. They are confused and horrified. Whether or not they are religious doesn't matter at all, you *must* celebrate Christmas! To not celebrate Christmas is.... it's just not human. So I've gone along. Of course I don't go to church or any of that silliness. There are plenty of Christmas fairy tales on television if I want to hear that kind of stuff. I give gifts and such. I go to family gatherings. That's about it I guess. I mean, what else is there?

The part that I cannot come to terms with is the money, the gift giving. Okay, let's say I agree that Christmas is about giving, love, and generosity and all that stuff. That's not a bad premise, after all. But how do we celebrate and put into action these noble ideas? We buy *rich people* gifts. And by rich I don't mean millionaires. I mean people that *don't need* these gifts. Like me. That's how we celebrate love? Factor in the religious aspects and I ask "That's how we celebrate the birth of God in human form? We buy people that have lots of things.... *more things?!*" Does that make sense to you at all? How many people in the world right now are poor? How many are starving? How many could use a meal, some clothes, or shelter? I mean *really use* these things. Need them. Let's not give to these poor souls, no. Jim needs some new floor mats for his car. Donna needs a new purse. Chris needs a hundred dollar video game. Kate needs a new iPhone. Brianna needs something—anything—with a diamond on it. So Christmas is about love and giving and caring and compassion, but only for your closest relatives? Does that sound all that compassionate to you? It's quite pathetic and we should be a little ashamed. What do you suppose Jesus would say about that? And what would he say about this Black Friday nonsense? People lining up for days, crushing each other against store doors, and trampling, running, and fighting—and literally dying—to get 'great deals' on stupid shit no one really needs. Every year you hear about at least one person being trampled to death during these stampedes of stupidity. Last year a young Wal-Mart employee was trampled to death after unlocking the doors. Compassion. Giving. Family. Peace. Yup, we got a lock on that stuff. I'm betting Jesus would say, "Yes! That's exactly how my birthday should be celebrated!"

Here's my take on it all (because I know you're dying to know). I think Christmas should be for the needy and children. I certainly wouldn't want to take Christmas away from children. (Do you really think I'm that cruel?) No, we should keep all that stuff: Santa and the fun and magic and stories and presents—but not too many presents. Jesus Crackers, have you seen the amount that kids get nowadays? It's embarrassing. I will not allow it. If a few close relatives want to give my child a gift, fine. A gift. But my floor will not be hidden by the endless amount of boxes for her to unwrap. It's not necessary, it's not good for the child, and the money could be better spent on someone that needs it.

So, yes, I have no problem with giving my child (or my nieces and nephews) Christmas gifts. But I certainly don't want anything from them. Same goes for their parents or any other adult. It's just silliness. A close relative recently asked me what I wanted for Christmas and I said, "Nothing." I wasn't being polite and coy or anything. I actually don't want *anything*. I mean, what do I need? Nothing. I said, "Look. If you insist on getting me something why don't you take the money that you were going to spend and donate it to the SPCA?" She looked at me like I was insane. But I was serious. I'd love knowing that some money went to the SPCA. That would make me feel good. That would feel like love and compassion. Much more so than me getting something I really don't need. [One relative did end up giving to the SPCA in my name. It was great. *Useful.*] I just think most people go overboard with their gift giving. An adult giving other adults Christmas gifts is just a weird idea to me. In-laws, coworkers, cousins, neighbours, etc. It's enough. Let the kids have it. Let the needy have it. Magic for the children and necessities for the needy, how's that for a Christmas idea? Helping people or animals in need while letting our children enjoy the fun and excitement of the holiday. Crazy idea?

In our culture? Yes. Yes it is.

<u>Magic Water</u>

It's your child. You have every right to sprinkle magic water on its head to open up the flow of "grace" from God to your baby's heart (yes, that's what you're doing). You have every right to do that. But isn't too much to expect someone not to giggle at the stupidity of it all?

It's also not lost on me that not one parent—not one—has even attempted to explain to me why they had their child baptized. Do they *have* to explain themselves to me? Of course not. But I tell you this, if I believed that magic water somehow made my child better, or benefited her in some manner, you can be damn sure I'd have no problem explaining why I believed such a thing.

<u>Mars, God, and Taxes</u>

I was leafing through the newest *National Geographic* magazine when I came across an article about Mars. I asked my 10 year old niece, who was visiting, if she learned anything about Mars in school. She said yes, but not much. After showing her a few pictures taken by the newest Mars rover she suddenly asked, "Do you believe in God or the Big Bang?"

I hesitated. In my head I was saying, *The Big Bang has been proven. It's not a matter of belief at this point.* I also thought the two weren't mutually exclusive. But out loud I simply replied, "The Big Bang." She said, "So you don't believe God made us?"

I looked at her, mildly surprised she didn't already know the answer, and said, "Well, no. Because I don't believe in God."

Her mouth literally hung open as she stared at me, *"Wwwhat?"*

I laughed at her reaction and said, "No, I don't believe in God. Is that surprising to you?" Still staring and looking slightly dazed, she said, "Yeah. I've never *heard* of anyone not believing in God." She sat back, dumbfounded. "How can.... how can anyone not love *God?*"

I said, "Well, I don't love God because I don't believe there is one. Alison and I both—we don't believe in God." Her eyes opened wide again. I said, "It's no big deal. Do you remember our wedding? It wasn't in a church and we were married by the mayor, not a minister. That's why. I'm surprised this is so surprising to you. You've really *never* heard of anyone that didn't believe in God?"

"No, never," she said, slowly shaking her head. "But... if you don't believe in Jesus... you won't have *Christmas.*"

I laughed, "Well, I go along with Christmas, but no, I don't believe in Jesus and all that."

She looked confused for a moment. Then she said, "But if there was no God, how do we have Christmas?" She straightened up and smiled. "Answer that. Prove me wrong." She folded her arms and sat back, looking quite satisfied.

I said, "Umm, no. I don't think Aunt Allie will be too pleased if I tried to prove you wrong. Look, you keep believing like you do. Don't worry about us."

Mind you, I was well aware I was on fragile ground here. I've never discussed this stuff with someone so young. I never wanted to. I'll not lie, I knew they were planning on getting her "confirmed" soon, and that bugged the hell out of me. But I'm not that stupid. I knew that causing any conflict in this manner would lead to more headaches than I would ever care to take on. In a few years, when she's a bit older, sure, I'd gladly discuss it all with her, if she so wished. But I won't be the one to bring it up.

I told her again, "So it's not a big deal. There are millions of people that don't believe. It's not unusual. But you do and that's fine. We just don't." She still looked devastated and confused.

I tried to change the subject. I'm not sure what I said next but within two minutes we were discussing taxes. She was quite angry when she learned that everyone has to pay taxes. Quite angry indeed.

104

Meatlessness Is Next To Godliness

People around here weep at the sight of meat on Good Friday. Seriously, show them a T-bone and they start bawling. Fish they'll gobble up before it's even off the hook. But beef? Forget about it. They're terrified of it. But just on that day. The other 364 days they'll bite the face off a live cow, are you kiddin'? But on Good Friday, no way. Not allowed to have it. Do they know *why* they're not allowed to have it? I've yet to meet one who has.

Anyway, I was again reading about early Christianity and it occurred to me that Maundy Thursday doesn't seem to mean dick-all to people around here. Why not? People usually love food-related traditions, and Jesus & Pals had the Last Supper on that day. So you'd figure we'd be commemorating it somehow. But nope. Not a word. But even more than that, how come I hear nothing about Ascension Day? Forty days after Easter, Jesus' buddies saw him fly up and away and into heaven. Literally. No, really. *Literally.* He flew away. Like a pelican. But no one mentions that around here. You'd figure there would be something said about that occasion too. Seems like a big day in the life of Jesus. But no one seems to care. Maybe we should celebrate it somehow. Maybe commemorate it with a new tradition or a rule. How about... oh, I don't know... you're not allowed to eat any birds that day. No chicken, no turkey, no goose—nothing with wings. We could say that because Jesus flew, used flight on that day, we honour him by "eating not from a winged beast." Doesn't that sound like it could catch on? Let's do it. So... spread the word.

No birds on Ascension Day!

Obsession – By John Calvin

More than once I've heard, "For an atheist you sure are preoccupied with religion." My usual response is, "That's why I'm an atheist—because I'm interested in religion."

Really, that's what eventually led to my being an atheist—my interest in religion. I was a believer. And I was such a believer that the details mattered to me. I wanted to know what I was supposed to know and I wanted to know that what I believed was *correct*. Of course, I now realize that asking such questions and having such expectations of your faith will inevitably lead one to reason that very little in religion makes sense. There are few answers and the ones there are are utterly ridiculous when examined with rational thought. So even as my faith dwindled, my interest in religion remained. Increased even. I became fascinated by the whole concept: crazy stories with little or no evidence of their validity, and literally billions of people accepting them without question, and even making decisions, rules, and laws based on these weird old tales. People kill and die because of these wacky myths. And anyone that questions this worldwide gullibility is mistrusted and disliked. How in the world is that not interesting?

Many people equate being an atheist to hating religion, or wanting nothing at all to do with religion, or even not wanting to discuss or acknowledge religion. This is yet another instance of how the simple concept of atheism is so often misunderstood. Are all atheists interested in religion in the way that I am? No. Some are interested, some are not. Pretty much like believers, really. Some are devout and go to church and learn about their particular religion or denomination, while others "just believe" and leave it at that. I just happen to be a person that finds religion—all religions—fascinating. Not *because* I'm an atheist, but because I'm fascinated by human behavior; behavior of all kinds, but especially those which make little sense to me and/or defy logic. And religion is the definitely the biggest and best example of such behaviour.

Take John Calvin, the 16th century French Protestant reformer and theologian who remains influential to this day. He stated that the authenticity of the Scriptures was made evident by—you guessed it—the Scriptures! Essentially, he said that the fact that the Scriptures said they were real is proof that the Scriptures are real. That's some kind of logic. He also believed that humans were created by God and put into two different categories. These categories determined whether you were going to end up in heaven or hell. *The Elect* were the chosen ones that were predestined for heaven and eternal salvation. Then there were *the Reprobates*. These folks were predestined to suffer everlasting damnation. Note the word *predestined*. This shit, according to our friend Johnny, was decided long before any of us existed, and there is nothing anyone can do to change it. A *Reprobate,* he said, can do nothing but good deeds, live a devout and holy life, and even reach "inner salvation", and God will still not give a shit. *He* knows what you really are. Once a *Reprobate* always a *Reprobate*. It should be noted as well that Calvin said *the Elect* could never fall from grace. Never. They can murder, cheat, and steal, and it doesn't matter one iota, for they are on their way to heaven. Convenient for *the Elect*, huh? And 500 years after his death, John Calvin is not looked at as the nutter he was. In fact, he's still quite admired and influential. How is that *not* interesting?

I've been accused of being "obsessed" with religion by two different people. One was a high-strung conspiracy nut, and the other, a holistic hippie. What's funny is that I never get accused of being obsessed about anything else, even though there are many things that hold my interest more. Things like music, the mafia, writing, language, World War II, astronomy, nature and animals, etc. In fact, I've written more about language than I have about religion, yet no one has ever said, "Why are you so obsessed with language?" Also, I'm quite confident in assuming that these arrogant folks would not accuse their religious relatives of being "obsessed". No, they save the insults for nonbelievers.

<u>An Open Letter</u>

[Many people outside Canada and the US may not know that in every hotel room you will find a Holy Bible resting inside the bedside table drawer. They have "been placed here by The Gideon's." Now who or what the Gideon's are is a whole other matter. Just know that I've never been in a hotel room that did not have a Bible in it.]

Thank you.

All you did was scribble a few words on a little pamphlet tucked inside a hotel Bible. It really seems like nothing. Actually, I'm sure many would say what you did was wrong or even disrespectful. But to me it was wonderful. It instantly put me in a great mood. Your comments like "This sounds like witchcraft" and "Yeah, let's indoctrinate our children even more" were actually inspiring. Why? It's simple really. Because they let me know there are others out there.

I know the western world is becoming less religious (except for the United States—I have no idea what the hell is going on down there), and that's great. But you see, most of the people around us (around me, anyway) are still completely tolerant of the nonsense; they even *respect* it. And there's not much sadder to me than when agnostics and atheists pander to religious people with the "I totally respect your beliefs" garbage.

Bullshit! Grow some balls! I'm not saying you should yell at every believer or be mean to them. I'm saying that any time they want to spout off about their superstitious nonsense, or try to make you believe, or try to spread their special brand of guilt, or homophobia, or racism, or whatever, have the guts to say, "You know what? That doesn't make any sense." That's it. You would do it for any other type of bullshit they might get on with. You'd have no problem telling them their belief that George Bush is really a 7-foot reptilian creature is insane, right? (Look it up. There are people that believe that.) But because they're Christian and believe in talking snakes you "respect" them. Get real. It's time we grew up as a culture, no? Atheists that argue for believer's rights get on my nerves only because it goes without saying that a person has a right to believe whatever their brain tells them is true. But they don't have the right to think the rest of the world should accept, bend, change, accommodate, enforce, or agree with their baseless ideas.

The great philosopher and cognitive scientist Daniel Dennett said that when writing his book *Breaking the Spell: Religion as a Natural Phenomenon* he tested people's reactions along the way and caught a lot of flak. Angry flak. So to be 'nicer' he made adjustments. But he said "it didn't do any good because I still got hammered for being 'rude and aggressive' and I came to realize that... religions have contrived to make it impossible to disagree with them, critically, without being rude." I've experienced first-hand how true this statement is. If you question someone's beliefs or even a religion in general, you are being mean, aggressive, and disrespectful. It really doesn't matter how you question it because all questions are inherently wrong and are simply not supposed to be asked. How lovely for these people to be so protected! It's disheartening to me when decent, rational people bow to this sentiment and apologize for doing or saying something that they need not apologize for.

Back to you, my dear hotel pal. I have a Flying Spaghetti Monster decal in the back window of my car. I keep this little guy there not because I think it'll change anything. It won't. But what it might do is make some non-believer who is familiar with the symbol say, "Hey, look at that; someone else around here who is tired of the bullshit." That's it. That's why it's there and that's exactly what I felt when I read your comments in that hotel room.

I thought to myself, "Progress." It was a lovely thought.

Once in a while I hear that someone I barely know, like a distant relative for instance, is an atheist. To be honest it always makes me happy. Any time I hear that reason and rationality is gaining ground I like it. And that's what your comments told me. And for that I thank you.

Opiniondemic

This is worth repeating a million times.

Just because you have an opinion, and just because you are entitled to your opinion, it does not mean your opinion is correct or as equally valid as anyone else's. Got that? People are trying so hard to be politically correct nowadays that they are ignoring the fact that, quite often, there is a **right** and a there is a **wrong**.

An example: Today I was strolling around a bookstore when I noticed a book called *The Illustrated History of the World*. It was one of those over-sized books that look like they are geared toward young kids. It's the kind of thing I would have loved as a child. I picked it up and turned to the first page. Know where it started? Why, it started at the beginning of the world of course, 6000 years ago. I'm serious. This is totally true. I was shocked. It was actually quite funny. I leafed through the book, from the creation of the world 6000 years ago (there were already people living in Newfoundland 6000 years ago, which is when Adam and Eve apparently popped into existence), to the pre-flood humans (which looked like what most people might think of as 'cave men'), to the flood, and on to other biblical accounts of events that probably didn't happen. I think teaching this stuff to children and calling it history is wrong, plain and simple. Factually wrong and morally wrong. Don't teach children opinion about things of which we have factual evidence to the contrary.

This phony 'history' is held as truth by some people; I get that. But it's their *opinion* that the earth is 6000 years old. These people, and their opinion, are wrong. It's as simple as that. It's a proven scientific fact that the earth is much older, 4.5 billion years old, as it were. Oh, they're entitled to their opinion, yes, I know, *I know*, for Jesus' sake, I know, but they're still wrong. Many people seem to have a problem with that concept. But it's easy. Some things, many things, more than you care to admit, are either right or wrong. They either are or are not. I know that hurts but that's the way it is. Either Bigfoot exists or it does not. (For some reason I wanted to write "he" instead of it.) Either the earth is flat or it is not. Either the earth is 6000 years old or it is not. Of course, some things are subjective and not so easily declared right or wrong. But that should go without saying. But then again, a lot of things should go without saying, yet I find myself having to say them. Over and over.

People just love using the phrase, "Well, that's my opinion" in debates, arguments, and discussions. It's often connected to "and I'm entitled to my opinion" or "Everyone's entitled to their opinion." It's the refuge of a person unequipped to keep up with the discussion and wanting out. I most often hear these useless statements uttered in reference to the God Question. "Well, I believe God exists and he created the world and that is my opinion and I am entitled to it because everyone is entitled to their opinion."

Absolutely. Couldn't agree more. But it adds nothing to such a discussion. Over time people have been led to believe that all opinions and beliefs are equally weighted. Nothing could be further from the truth. Here's an example: I was discussing this very subject (the God Question) with a man and a woman, both believers. At one point the woman got frustrated and triumphantly stated, "Well, it's my *belief* that the Bible is true!" She stressed the word belief as if it would render my argument invalid. I responded, "Yes, but all the facts point to that being wrong." The man that was with us immediately burst into laughter. He looked at me like I was a moron and said, "How can someone's *belief* be wrong?" Then they both started to laugh. I said, "Hitler had lots of beliefs. Do you think any of them were wrong?" Hitler had an opinion about Jewish people. Would you, Silent Reader, say it was a true opinion? Was he entitled to that opinion? Would you say it was valid? Would you say it was just as valid as anyone else's? Here's the answer in case you're confused: Hitler was indeed entitled to his opinion. But his opinion was not valid. It was not true, and he was not entitled to act upon his opinion just because he was entitled to it. Let me go out on a limb here, being the daring outside-the-box thinker that I am, and say that Hitler's beliefs and opinions about Jewish people were.... wrong. People used to be of the opinion that the earth was flat. Were they entitled to that opinion? Yes sir. Was their opinion wrong? You betcha. People used to believe that the sun revolved around the earth. Were they entitled to that belief? They sure were. Was that belief wrong? Sweet silly Moses, yeah. People used to think Lance Armstrong was a great guy with a natural gift for athletic excellence. Were they entitled to that opinion? Of course. Was that opinion wrong? Super wrong.

I know I'm belaboring the point here, and it's such a simple concept, but I see with my own eyes and hear with my own ears so many people that just don't get it. Political correctness has taught us that everyone should be heard. Well, that's only true to an extent. Everyone should be heard, yeah, but some should only be heard from once. Some ideas have been adequately debunked. You can have your opinion that the moon is actually a camera lens trained on the earth so Spanky the Evil Hamster Overlord can spy on us from a parallel universe, you're entitled to that. Just don't expect any rational person to treat it as valid or plausible unless you have some evidence.

<u>Our Phony, Who Art in Heaven</u>

Let's stop giving Jesus so much praise just because he was whipped for a while.

There are people in the world this very instant that are going through worse than what he supposedly went through. Much worse. Plus, many of these people will endure their pain much longer than what he did. He actually didn't endure it long at all. Julia Sweeney said, "Jesus had a really bad weekend." And let's not forget that while Jesus was the son of God (a concept I still find funny—that God is a single dad), he was also God himself. So what happened was God let himself get tortured and killed. So what? He's God! You think he feels pain? Nah, of course not. And even if he did I'm supposed to feel bad for him? A guy that created millions of humans—without their consent, by the way—that have also felt such pain? *He* had a choice; humans did not. *He* chose that 'sacrificing his only son' plan; we did not. And besides that, God is eternal right? He's been around for an eternity! He'll be around for an eternity! That's forever! What's a couple of days of pain in eternity's terms? It's like a fuckin' nanosecond!

May I suggest that God didn't even feel pain when he was being whipped and nailed to the cross? May I suggest he was faking it, just to make the story better so people would be more likely to feel sorry for him, thus feeling guilty about and subsequently appreciating his self-sacrifice? May I suggest that because he's God and he knows all, he knew that Mel Gibson was going to make a film that would actually sway the weakest-minded people of our society into guilt-ridden belief, so he simply faked the whole thing?

Well, that is indeed what I am suggesting. God faked the

115

whole thing—the screaming, the crying, and even the wincing. All fake.

That's right, Silent Reader; God's a big fat phony.

Petri Souls

You people that believe in souls, let me ask you something. At what point does a person actually get a soul? Is it when they are born? When they are conceived? When they are baptized? When they are old enough to vote? See, the problem is that pinning down an actual point where a person, or an embryo or a fetus, gets their soul, is not only impossible, it completely lacks logic.

Pro-lifers like to say that a person is a person at the moment of conception. The particularly religious pro-lifers seem to feel that, since this little speck of cells is a person, he or she already has their soul intact. Okay, but what about fertilized eggs that are flushed out of the woman's body during her menstrual cycle? It happens a lot. Just because a sperm fertilizes an egg it does not mean there will be a pregnancy. Just think about it. Billions of women all over the world are releasing tiny little people with tiny little souls out of their bodies far too soon to make it on their own. How is a fertilized egg supposed to support itself in this crazy world? I would assume, according to these right wing religious pro-lifers, these women are committing involuntary manslaughter.

Let's say the little soulful egg doesn't get flushed out. Let's say it wins the embryonic lottery, snags itself a sperm, travels down the Fallopian tube and implants itself in the uterus. When does that embryo get its soul? The stem cell debate centers around the use of 3-day-old embryos called blastocysts. Opponents of such research say we cannot destroy these blastocysts because they are people. A blastocyst is made up of 150 cells. Do you realize how small that is? Neuroscientist Dr. Sam Harris points out for comparison that the brain of a house fly is made up of 100,000 cells. Understand now how small a blastocyst is? *The brain of a housefly is over 650 times bigger than the cluster of cells needed for stem cell research!* Are these people actually suggesting that this little speck of cells that has no brain and no neurons is a person? It has a soul? So those little petri dishes in science labs are actually housing human souls? Well, if they die do they go to heaven? Do those little microscopic specks show up at the Pearly Gates?

According to some Christian denominations, a person cannot get into heaven if he/she dies before baptism because of Original Sin. So I guess that means those little cells clusters would go to hell, unless of course they were baptized. But that's not likely. Maybe there should be priests knocking on the doors of laboratories all over the world asking if they can baptize these doomed little cellular speckles. Since they can't very well dunk the blastocysts in a river or dab their nonexistent foreheads with holy water, I suppose they'd probably have to use little droppers for the ceremonies. Really, should we risk having these innocent 3-day-old cells end up in hell to be tortured for eternity. Hmm. How would the devil and his minions torture a cluster of microscopic cells anyway?

And another thing, embryos sometimes end up splitting, eventually developing into twins. Does the puny soul in this embryo also split? Are there already two souls in the embryo because they already know they're going to split? Imagine, two souls, two people, trapped together inside a microscopic clump of 150 cells. Tight quarters. And if you don't buy this tiny-cellular-soul idea, then when exactly do these soulless specks get their soul injections? And where does it come from? (God, right? How'd I know that? Smart, I suppose.) But there has to be a point where one second the cells are soulless and the next second soulful. Surely no one would suggest that the soul is something that develops slowly; that one can have just a little bit of soul. Because, as James Brown would tell you, "Ya either got soul or ya don't!"

Actually I have no idea what James Brown would say and that is not a real quote.

<u>Ping-Pong with Jesus</u>

There are a few things I dislike about being an atheist. One is how so many people complicate the concept, when it's about as simple as a concept can get. It's not "just another religion", it's not a belief system, and it's not one of the world's competing religious beliefs, because it's not a stance *of* faith, but rather a stance *on* faith. There's a huge difference.

Here's what I most often say when I'm asked why I'm atheist: "I see no reason to believe in a God." That's the gist. It's *why act as if something is true just because you can't prove it's false?* I can't prove flying hippos don't exist, so should I go around believing they do? Should I expect you to believe in flying hippos too? That's one of the dumbest statements I hear when discussing God—that we atheists cannot prove there is no God. Of course we can't, and we're not trying to. It's just a backward idea. Firstly, we're not the ones claiming that something exists. The burden of proof is on you, not us. Using the flying hippo example again, is it up to me to prove they don't exist? Obviously, the people claiming that hippos are flying around somewhere are the ones that need to demonstrate it. Secondly, just because something cannot be proven negatively, that does not mean that the affirmative is true. I cannot prove flying hippos, talking caterpillars, or cat-juggling ants don't exist. So does that mean that my stance (that these things do *not* exist) is equal-but-opposite to my opponent's argument (that these things *do* exist)? Any reasonable person would say, "Of course these are not equally valid arguments. One is making claims with no evidence, while the other is asking for evidence before they will be convinced." You should apply the exact same logic to the God Question! It's amazing to rational people that so many of you throw this logic away when it comes to religion. Critics also say that atheists are claiming, "I know there is no God" or "I know nothing happens after we die". These and similarly odd and unrelated assumptions are statements that no realistic or intelligent atheist would ever make. Is there a God or gods? I have no idea. I doubt it. There's certainly no reason to think there is. Do we live on in some form of consciousness after we die? No idea. Again, there's certainly no reason to think we do.

Possibly the funniest misconception about atheism is that we "hate God", or, even funnier, that we're Satan worshippers. (I worked with a woman that long knew my feelings about God and religion. I thought she understood it. But when she asked me one day, "I know you don't believe in God, but do you believe in the devil?" I realized she had no idea.) I am anti-God in the sense that I'm against the *idea* of God, and even more so, the way in which humans fall for the claim that he exists. But I don't hate God himself (herself? itself?) because I don't believe he's real. Knowing what I know about him (as a fictional character) I can safely say I do not like the character. But it's much like disliking Hannibal Lector, Claudius, or Nurse Ratchet. They are fictional characters with bad traits. They are bad people, but they aren't real! (Actually these characters are better in a very real sense because the damage done in their names is entirely fictional. I cannot say the same for God. The damage done in his name is all too real.) Recently some Christians posted some silly Facebook Share about how some evil atheists want to remove a cross from a 9/11 memorial. While it's true, a cross shouldn't be at such a memorial, I was more interested in the comments left by some confused Christians. One said, "People always want to blame God when something bad happens." The atheists aren't blaming God! How could they? They don't even believe in him! This was definitely a person that thinks that atheists are people that believe in God, but just hate him rather than worship him. It sounds stupid because it is, but I assure you, a lot of people think that's what atheists are: believers that hate God. The misconceptions about atheists are sadly quite common, and that's the first thing I hate about being an atheist.

My second gripe is with the labels some atheists choose to go by. Like *Freethinkers*. I don't like that term. I find it... a little presumptuous; a little pretentious. And a bit arrogant. I will admit there are times it's hard not to feel a little mentally superior when talking to someone that believes in talking snakes, but humility is a great asset when you're in conflict with someone, especially when that person is arrogant enough to think the Benevolent Creator of All Things cares deeply about them. Believers like to call atheists arrogant, but where's the logic in that? The real arrogance is claiming to know there is a God without any evidence to back it up; the real arrogance is to believe that you were made in God's image and that the universe was made for you and your kind. And to expect others to accept all that without question and to believe the same? Whoo-wee! That is arrogance off the charts! But the worst label is surely the *Brights*. These are a group of people that hold a "naturalistic view" of existence. It's a boastful, self-aggrandizing name. It amazes me that more than one person agreed to go by that label. Their stance is good. Their name is awful.

The third thing that bothers me about atheism needs a bit of a preamble about the idea of the afterlife. When I first realized how ridiculous the idea of God and gods were I naturally started to wonder about the afterlife as well. Some connect God with the afterlife far too tightly. I know this because almost every time someone hears I don't believe in God one of their first questions is, "So what happens after we die?" Sometimes I answer, "What does that have to do with God?" Why is it people cannot picture an afterlife without thinking God has to be involved? Why can't we just "move on" to somewhere else? Another dimension?

Another plane of existence invisible to the one we now occupy? Why do you need God to allow that to happen? People are so unimaginative! Other times I have responded with, "What happens after we die? Do you actually think that I—me—Brent MacLean, have figured out what happens after we die?"

The truth is that I think it's likely nothing. I don't know that of course, but I really don't see any valid reason to think anything else. (Ghosts, you say? Please. Don't you find it a tad odd that after all this time, after all the people that have lived and died, we still don't have a shred of conclusive evidence that tells us that ghosts are real?) Sometimes I think that our existence alone is reason enough to accept the *possibility* that there could be much more to our state of being, more than we could ever contemplate. It very well could be that way. But believe it? Nah, I don't. I'm certainly not going to live my life on the assumption that there is some kind of afterlife. And that's the difference between people like me and people like the religious. They want something to be true; they feel better thinking that it's true, so they go around acting as if it is true. I can't do that. I can't live as if something that probably isn't is, just because it sounds nicer. So after light pondering and serious thought I just cannot believe we're all going to turn into angels after we die. I don't believe your relatives are "watching over" you. It just doesn't add up, no matter how much it comforts people. See, I'm not concerned with comfort when to comes to finding out the truth about the world. I'm curious about the real state of things; what is and what is not. And believe me, the idea that after I die I have to spend my time "watching" over my relatives is enough to make me pray for no afterlife.

I get that the main reason people cling to ideas such as the afterlife, and by extension, the notion of a God, is simply a crippling fear of death. And I don't for a second think people fear death because they are afraid they are going to end up in hell. It's more that they are afraid of the unknown. And again, I totally understand that. It's a seemingly innate fear we have that our own existence is finite. People just want to believe that death is not the end; that it's merely a transitional step. I've had people flat-out tell me, "I don't want death to be the end. I want to keep going." I understand that desire. I don't have it myself though. The idea of existing "forever" in a conscious form is not an appealing one for me. And as I said, there's really no reason to believe that we do "keep going". I suspect being dead is a lot like the time before you were born. As Mark Twain said, "I do not fear death. I had been dead for billions and billions of years before I was born, and had not suffered the slightest inconvenience from it." You just don't exist, and you have no idea that you don't exist, because you don't exist! And if that is the case, if there is nothing after this life ends, what's so bad about that? What's so bad about thinking this life is the only one we get? "What's *good* about it?" I hear you asking. Well, you're more likely to appreciate every second you have on this earth if you think that it's the only life you'll ever get. It makes the here and now so much more precious. Just think of how lucky each of us is to have been born at all. I mean, the odds of it are astronomical.

As sad and tragic as early deaths are, if you consider the possibilities of how many different people could have been born, they are still examples of lucky people; lucky in the sense that they got here at all, statistically speaking. Don't for a second think I'm saying that people that die young should just be grateful they had any time alive at all. I'm not saying that. Okay? Do I need to repeat that part? Okay. *I'm not saying people shouldn't whine, cry, or complain about people dying young. I'm not saying it's not a bad thing and I'm not saying it's a good thing.* (Yes, Silent Reader, repeating this stuff is necessary.) I'm talking about the luck of existence. I'm talking about statistics, numbers, and odds.

The shock of realizing that there's no reason to believe in

an afterlife is something many people have a hard time dealing with. It's different for everyone. Some adapt quickly and easily roll with the idea that "you only live once", and immediately appreciate this life as the fleeting one-shot deal it likely is. I was like that, but only for a short while. And here is where I (finally) get to the third thing about my atheism that I do not like.

It's having to deal with jerks. See, while I can easily appreciate things more, such as time with my wife and daughter, beautiful weather, lovely naps, good food, great music, animals, etc.—all the things that life entails, I can't help but also think, *This is all we get. This is our only chance. When this life of mine is gone I'm gone. So why in the hell do I have to spend this fleeting time dealing with jerks? Why do I have to spend this momentary slice of existence dealing with morons and inconsiderate idiots? And why do I constantly have to do things I don't want to do? Work where I don't want to work? Participate in traditions I don't want to participate in?* The fact that I don't believe that when I die I'm gonna be playing ping-pong with Jesus doesn't bother me at all. I'm more bothered by the fact that outside forces (people) constantly screw up my **limited amount of time**. That's the sticking point for me. So little time, so many jerks.

So that is my biggest dislike about thinking the way I do. Would I change it if I could? Yeah, I'd care less about negative outside forces if I could, sure. Would I prefer to live as others do, believing this life is just one out of many? Would that alleviate this complaint? It might alleviate the complaint but I still would never want to live that way. It would be delusional. Yes, folks, if you believe we get another life just because that sounds nicer, then I'm afraid you are being delusional. In pretty much every other faction of life, except for God and heaven, people don't automatically believe what sounds better. They don't automatically believe what makes them feel nice. They might hope for it, but they don't believe it. And I'm not the kind of person that could trick himself into believing something anyway. I'm far too aware; I think too much. It's apparently why I'm not a good candidate for hypnosis. (Yes, I've done tests.) Believing in something without evidence is simply not an option for me.

Another, more minor thing that I don't really like is that I can no longer seriously entertain ideas of ghosts and demons and all the other supernatural stuff many people believe in. Things like the Bermuda Triangle, folklore tales of strange creatures terrorizing small towns, and hauntings and such— I used to love that stuff when I was a kid. In primary and elementary school I would often go to the library and head straight for the back corner where they kept a small collection of books about ghosts, Bigfoot, aliens, and all sorts of paranormal stuff. I didn't necessarily believe in all of it, but it all fascinated me. I *wanted* to believe in all of it. I loved the unknowns, the unexplained things; the idea that there were all kinds of stuff, strange and creepy stuff, all around us that weren't in plain sight. Of course, a side-effect of this interest was that I spent many a night in my bed completely terrified because I was sure there were ghosts knocking about in my house. Satan, spirits, random demons, the walking dead, angels—all of these things and more tortured me. My dad said, "There's no such thing as ghosts." But that wasn't enough to alleviate my fears. It made no sense. I thought *How can there be no ghosts when angels exist?* (My dad later told me and my brother that he didn't believe in angels. He said, and this is a quote, "You just go in the ground. When you're gone you're gone." That rocked my world. Freaked me the fuck out. But no, that was not the seed of my atheism, if that's what you're wondering. It was many years later that I rationalized my way to non-belief.) While these things terrified me at night I still loved it all in the daytime. But after learning to think more logically, weighing the likelihood of things and relying on evidence before making decisions, I just sort of lost interest in the paranormal and supernatural. I tried watching a show recently about small towns and their unique tales of ghosts and witches and stuff but....it's just not the same anymore. I can't help but think how silly it all is; how gullible the believers are. So I do miss that a little bit, the interest and entertainment I got from such fringe topics.

Besides those things—the misconceptions of what atheism actually means, the labels some atheists give themselves, the necessity of spending my very limited time on earth dealing with inconsiderate and selfish people, and the loss of a fun childhood interest and hobby—what I dislike most about atheism is the mistrust. I hate that people think we're strange, odd, or crazy. *We're* the crazy ones!

• We don't believe in talking snakes.

• We don't believe that a Jewish carpenter was murdered and three days later, woke up, walked around for a bit, and then flew up to heaven, body and all.

• We don't believe there's a God who gets pissed off if you eat pepper steak stir-fry on Good Friday.

• We don't believe there's a man in the sky that wants to be thanked before every meal. Well, not every meal. Not breakfast or lunch. I guess he's not paying attention then. Maybe God sleeps in.

• We don't believe that women can get pregnant without having sex or coming into contact with a male's sperm. We don't believe in virgin births.

• We don't believe there's a God that cares who wins the Grammy for Best Female Vocalist ("Alright, first I'd like to thank God for blessing me and without whom none of this would be happening...") yet at the very same time doesn't seem to care if scores of people starve to death on the other side of the world every single day.

• We don't believe an old man went around and gathered two of every animal species on earth, and built a boat big enough to house these millions and millions of animals while God flooded the world to kill everyone on it, men, women and children.

• We don't believe a man can live inside a whale.

• We don't believe people can walk on water.

• We don't believe the earth is only six thousand years old and that man and dinosaurs lived at the same time.

• We don't believe there's a loving and caring God that wants homosexuals put to death because a man lying with another man is an "abomination".

• We don't believe in talking donkeys.

• We don't believe that should a man find out that his new bride is not a virgin that he should bring her to her father's doorstep and kill her.

• We don't believe it's right to murder a man for collecting sticks on a Sunday, because that's just too much Sabbath work for God's liking.

• We don't believe that there's a God, a Supreme Being and Creator of all Things, who really wants us to slice the foreskin off the penises of baby boys.

• We don't believe that should a baby die before they get magic water splashed on their head they will spend eternity in hell.

We don't believe these things and we're the weird ones! I'll never understand that. And I don't like that. It's quite indicative of how backwards the world is; you ask for evidence before blindly following far-fetched claims and you are the odd one. I just cannot get used to it.

So there are indeed a few things I don't care for when it comes to atheism, but what's the alternative? I could be delusional and follow God's orders, which were actually made up by a bunch of unenlightened, stuffy, racist, sexist, sexually-repressed men some 2000-5000 years ago. Yeah, I could do that. But I'd rather remain a little more critical, a little more realistic, even with the difficulty of spending my limited time dealing with everything we have to deal with, with nothing to look forward to after this life is done. I have to accept that the world is the way it is and that I must do my best to filter out the negative while focusing on all that's positive. And to be honest, even if I still believed in God the whole thing would bug the hell out of me. I'd no doubt be thinking *Why did God make us so flawed? And why would he punish us for those very flaws? Free will? Well, why is it that he apparently chips in to help us from time to time? I've never met a believer that didn't believe that God helps us at times. And why does he help some but not others? Why would he help Johnny survive the hurricane while letting little Marcie die in the flood? If we're headed to heaven anyway, and he wants us to get to heaven why don't he just put us in heaven? Because I keep hearing that he loves us and wants us to go to heaven. If he loves us so much, why bother with all the tests, tests that we so often fail because of the flaws he instilled in us? Why bother with tests that, should we fail, will result in our being tortured and for eternity? That doesn't sound like love.*

How could I ever ignore the flaws in that kind of logic? While being an atheist isn't always peachy, it's both automatic and better than the alternatives.

By the way, if I were to play ping-pong with Jesus I'd slaughter him.

Playing God
(A Healthy Dose of the Abyss)

Playing God. What a stupid phrase that is. It's only dragged out when some self-righteous enemy of progress is worried that someone might be making their own non-church mandated decision. You often hear it about cloning. "Scientists shouldn't bring the woolly mammoth back—that's playing God." I say, "Nuts to that! I'd love for them to bring the woolly mammoth back. Why not? What's it to you?"

You also hear it about stem cell research. "We shouldn't play God and hurt that clump of cells! That's a baby!" I say, "get real, that's not a baby, it's a cluster of cells. And do you know how many *actual living* people such research will benefit?" You gotta know that if any one of these cell lovers had a close family member with a terminal disease that could potentially be cured through research on stem cells they'd change their tune pretty damn quick. "Sorry, Jim Bob, I know your daughter is dying and we could save her by destroying this cluster of cells that is smaller than an insect's brain, but you know, like you said before, this is a *baby*. Therefore your daughter is no more important than this microscopic bit of protoplasm. According to *you.*"

You probably most often hear this phrase used when talking about euthanasia, doctor-assisted suicide, or whatever name you wish to call it. It's the 'right to die' debate. It should go without saying that I believe a person should be able to decide when and how they die. You have a terminal illness and your last days—or years—will be miserable and pain-filled? By all means, check out if you wish. Some people would rather these patients suffer, all the while knowing things will never get better? That's about as cruel as you can get, if you ask me. These pro-pain people always bring up ridiculous scenarios where people are killing off their elderly relatives or doctors are just injecting people with a healthy dose of the abyss just for the hell of it. What, you don't think that whole process can be strictly regulated and monitored? It can and it can be done very easily.

But here's my point with all this: The idea of us 'playing God' is nonsense. They say we're playing God if we resurrect an extinct species. Well, what if we're responsible for the extinction of that species in the first place? I mentioned woolly mammoth. One of the reasons they died out was because they were hunted so extensively by humans. The Great Auk would no doubt be strolling around today if it weren't for our love of their down. I'm sure I could come up with lots of species that we've killed with our pollution and habitat destruction, but my point is that if bringing an animal back is playing God, then so too is killing them off. So stop hunting. You have no right. It's playing God.

They say stem cell research is playing God because a little clump of cells gets destroyed in the process. Okay, but what about all medical care? Should we really be going against God's design and giving little Braden Aiden Hayden Caden Jayden a bone marrow transplant? God obviously created this boy with bone marrow that totally sucks. Should we play God and mess with his all-knowing and all-loving design? What about diabetes? Obviously God didn't think Mr. Shikidance deserved to enjoy sugar like the rest of us, so why should we be playing God and giving him access to insulin? If you believe in this *natural equals God* nonsense then any interference by us and our technology is playing God. Not letting things play out on their own and going against the natural state of things is playing God, according to that logic.

They say it's playing God to give in to poor Uncle Dill's wishes and pull his plug even though he's dying a horrible death. Well, wasn't it playing God when we plugged him in in the first place? Why do they get to decide when it's okay to interfere with nature and when it's not?

Here's my theory. I think the answer has something to do with how close the issue affects you, the person making the stand. If it's between your daughter and a little blob of cells then I'm willing to bet you'd think it's just fine. It's only a speck of goo on a slide, right? How can we compare that to your living, breathing daughter? And if you were the one in agony and you could not handle the pain anymore then by all means play God and start yankin' some plugs. Am I correct in these assumptions? I believe I am. I believe it's callousness on the part of the protester and it's because the issue is detached from them; it doesn't really affect them. It's a lack of sympathy and a total lack of empathy. And is that any way to regulate something as important as life and death? Is that any way to show compassion for those that know only suffering?

Pre-emptive Prayer

There was yet another mass murder in the United States yesterday. By the time you read this there will undoubtedly have been many more, so the details aren't worth going over here. But people are injured, people are dead. It's terrible. And of course everyone is keeping those affected in their prayers at the moment. Hey. Here's a suggestion for you "thoughts and prayers" people. It's also for you "please pray for those affected" people. The masses that love to say "God bless those lost", I'm speaking to you as well.

Why don't you do this: Since you believe in all that prayer stuff, why don't you all get together and have a big ol' prayer session—one of your useful prayer chains—and ask God to stop letting these things happen in the first place? I mean, you know, instead of praying for his help *after* the damage has been done and the lives have been lost. You obviously believe he has the power to control whatever he wants down here or you wouldn't pray in the first place, so ask him to pre-emptively stop all these natural and man-made tragedies, so then everything will be fine and peaceful, no one will suffer and die, and you won't have to pray on a nearly constant basis for people facing hardships. He's a loving and caring God right? He loves us all you say, so I'm sure he'll be up for that idea.

Promised Prayers Pending

Nowadays when someone loses a loved one they get flooded with messages on Facebook and Twitter assuring the mourners that "you're in my prayers". Setting aside my thoughts on the pointlessness of prayer, I can't help but wonder how many people actually do pray for the people in mourning.

Think about it. You've probably said it to someone yourself. "So sorry for your loss. You're in my thoughts and prayers," or "My condolences. I will say a prayer for you and your family," or something similar. But I'm willing to bet that very few of you actually got down on your knees soon after and sent God a well-constructed prayer which included some kind of request for your grieving acquaintance. I'm sure some smart-asses are now saying, "I don't *have* to get on my knees to pray!" Okay, fine. Take out the kneeling. Stand up. I'm still willing to bet you didn't have a real heart-to-heart with God like you said you would. I just wonder how many of those promised prayers are actually prayed. About 1%, I betcha. People love those empty gestures. Saying "you're in my prayers" *is* the act of condolence. And even if you did get around to praying to Jesus for your recently saddened friend, what is it you ask? To what, make their suffering not as.... insufferable? To ask God to consider letting the departed person into heaven? I never understood this tendency to pray to God *after* something bad happens, but I've written about that elsewhere. All I'm saying here is that there are surely millions of promised prayers that never went fulfilled. I wonder what God would say about you handing out those empty prayer promises so casually. He'd probably say, "Hey. Don't."

Brent MacLean

Purgatory Skippage

[The following is a message from a friend of mine, along with my response. It really strikes at the heart of what some people, atheists included, have a hard time with when it comes to belief in God and an afterlife. Knowing we're going to die is a heavy burden to carry for most people, religious or not.]

Friend:

So Carey's brother died yesterday. He knew he was dying. They gave him 3 weeks; it was 3 weeks ago to the day. He declined hospital treatment and chose to die at home, which would be my wish as well in that position.

Anyway, he's Italian-Catholic and really religious. Before he died, while he was still lucid, his priest performed some sort of mass that is supposed to allow you to skip purgatory and go straight to heaven. It was after he chose to die at home, and requested everyone come see him. It was like a wake, except he was lying there alive while people lined up to say goodbye. It was actually less awkward than if there was a dead body in the room. All everyone talked about was how he was going to skip purgatory. It was so weird; people were all excited, like he won a trip to Disneyland or something. When I talked to him to say goodbye, he was laughing and joking around. He wasn't the least bit afraid. And all his family were actually excited for his purgatory skippage.

Of course, I thought it was all hokum. But it was amazing to see what a comfort religion actually can be in a time like that. And as much as I enjoy rational thinking and sanity, I actually envy the ability of those who believe like that.

Anyway, full-on Italian-Catholic funeral mass tomorrow. Not sure if you've ever had the pleasure, but if only five people try to crawl into his coffin with him and wail for God to take them too, then it will be considered tame by Italian funeral standards. Should be interesting.

My response:

I've sometimes wondered if I'd be better off believing in something so wholeheartedly that something like death wouldn't bother me at all. I can see why it would be nice. But I really can't do anything about it, even if I wanted to. Some people just ask questions automatically, and since we do we just cannot accept those ideas, even if they might help us feel better during tough times. I suppose it's the whole 'ignorance is bliss' idea. I think it's definitely true to a degree. It's kind of why I stopped paying attention to the news and such lately. I just don't want to know what is going on anymore.

I've never been to an Italian funeral, but I have been to a few Catholic funerals. I always hated them for two reasons. The main reason is that in every Catholic funeral I've been to they talked far more about Jesus than they did about the person that died. It really bugged me. Fine, say a few words about Jesus and God, but try to honour the person that just passed too, you know? It should be about the person more than anything else. The second thing I didn't like is that they were really long, which really wouldn't have bothered me if they focused on the person. But since it was all about Jesus it got real irritating. I said to my wife after the last one we attended, "Whose funeral was that—Elaine's or Jesus'?"

But even though religion and superstitious belief can comfort some in hard times, I really believe that religion, as a whole, does far more damage than good. I also think people would be more likely to do good things and appreciate their lives more if they thought that this was the only life we get. And it always boils down to that one notion for me: What *is* and what is *not*. I just cannot ignore logic, even in stressful times.

<u>Raining in Paradise</u>

The idea of paradise has always struck me as funny, both in a concrete and abstract, mythical sense (such as the Garden of Eden or heaven). The only way for paradise to actually work is if all the people there felt and thought exactly the same way about it. For instance, most people picture a beautiful sunny scene. Most would probably say their idea of paradise would include a warm or hot climate. Well, guess what. Sun and heat are certainly not *my* idea of paradise. A paradise can only be a paradise if it is a *personal* paradise. There's no way you're going to get more than five people to agree on what would make a place and time paradise.

You could say that, with it being paradise and all, everyone would simply enjoy whatever it entailed, that their minds would be altered to enjoy whatever situation paradise offered them, but that would be taking liberties with the idea, and it would certainly open a whole jar of silliness that I'm not going to entertain here. I actually discussed this *personal paradise* idea and the inevitable conflicts such a concept would create in a paper I wrote for a Christianity course I took in University, although I can't remember the exact context. So.....

Um..... huh.

Lost my train of thought. I bet that never happens in paradise.

<u>Right Next to Me</u>

I get that you believe there's some sort of higher power. I get that you insist that there must have been a creator because you can't understand how "all this" came to be without someone designing it. I think your logic is flawed but I get how you got there. What I don't get is how you settled on a particular God to worship. I asked one woman this very question a few years ago, when she told me that she believed in God. I said, "Well, which God do you believe in?" At first she looked confused. Then she said, "I thought there *was* only one God." I told her that there were actually thousands of different gods that people believed in throughout history and how there are still many different gods one can choose from. So I just wanted to know why, out of all the possibilities, she decided that her God (the Christian God) was the "one true God". She squirmed uncomfortably and said, "Well... I don't know.... that's just what we were told."

Amazing, isn't it? Because that's what it all boils down to, folks. People just jump into the pool of superstitious beliefs in which their parents swam. There's no questioning, no shopping around for the 'right' God, no effort to discover which God might be more likely to exist. Truth is just not an issue for these people; not even a passing thought! It's simply "that's what we were told." I'm glad people use a little more rationality when deciding other things. Can you imagine what the world would be like if we all just automatically believed what we were told by those in our general vicinity? If we never thought for ourselves or used logic to figure out the truth about things? What a static, stagnant, stalled, and broken-down world it would be, which really makes sense because that is in fact what religion aims to do: It tells us that they already have all the answers, that there's no need to search for anything else. I don't ever want to be so stunted, so restricted. New ideas, new facts, and growth—these are all enemies of the religious mind. And the religious mind is the enemy of reason and knowledge. To tell a child that learning about how the earth was created, and how life as we know it came to be, is pointless because the Bible already tells us that God made the earth, man, donkeys and dinosaurs all in six days is doing that child a great disservice. Teaching a child to question things is a good thing, not a bad thing. Teaching them to question everything except one thing is a *confusing* thing.

So again I ask you, how did you decide which god to follow? Surely it wasn't simply determined by where you happen to have been born. Surely you wouldn't just do whatever the people in your geographical area told you to do. You have your own mind, right? Certainly when it comes to matters of such importance as the Almighty Creator, heaven, and eternal salvation you'd be a little more discerning and do your due diligence to be as sure as you can be that you didn't pick the wrong god. Because you must remember, all religions can't be correct. In fact, if one happened to be right, that means the rest are wrong. Out of all the options available, what makes you so confident that you haven't picked a false god, a false god that the *real* God will burn you for worshipping? Because according to most of the world's still-prevalent gods, you, a person believing in a false god, are no different than me, a person believing in no god. So we have the same fate, you and I. Funny to think, isn't it? You're laughing at me because I'm destined to burn in hell, all the while not realizing that the real God is reserving a place for you in the fire as well—right next to me.

See ya there!

<u>Spiritual Sellout</u>

A coworker told me that one of the Columbine shooters crouched down and asked a girl hiding under a desk if she still believed in God. She said yes. Then he shot her.

My coworker said, "Even *you* gotta admit, that's really cool, standing up for you beliefs like that." It's as if I was supposed to be in awe of this girl. If this story is true, and it probably isn't, I'm not in awe at all. First of all, if she was a believer, I would think she should have been asking herself, "Where the hell is God? Why isn't he *stopping this?*"

Second of all, if the point of this story was that the shooter *wanted* her to say no, then I would say it was foolish to not go along with what the shooter wanted. I'm sure that God, if he's at all a nice guy, would have looked the other way if the girl told some psycho asshole kid that she wasn't a believer so he wouldn't murder her. Maybe not. Maybe I'm wrong. Maybe that would have pissed God off. *"I don't care if you're about to be shot in the head or you're being tortured or your child is being tortured! Don't you EVER say you don't believe in me!"* Then again, who knows? Read your Bible. It shows pretty clearly what a horrendous dick God can be. Of course, the psycho would have probably shot her anyway, no matter what she answered.

People have such a weird thing about standing up for your beliefs. They twist a noble idea into something pointless. I'm not saying you should sell yourself out and betray your values and your sense of decency and honour to save your life. I'm not saying anyone should do *anything* to save themselves. I'm saying that in this situation, telling a lie to a maniac is no big deal. And I'm certainly not saying you should lie to please believers. I constantly say the opposite. I regularly encourage people to stand up for themselves and to not shy away from speaking out against the injustices and hypocrisies of religious belief. I can't stand the non-believers that cower whenever believers start talking. That's one of the main goals of my writing: to encourage rational people to speak out against bullshit they know in their hearts they should denounce. But this (hypothetical) Columbine scenario is a whole different thing. It's life and death. Because I gotta tell ya, if a wacky Christian showed up at my gym with a rifle and started gunning down people because he thought they were infidels, and he asked me if I believed in God, you better believe I'd say, "Of course I believe in God." I'd be an idiot not to. What would it prove if I said, "Nah, man. I don't believe in God. I think it's a load of shit"? What would that accomplish?

And I'm pretty sure that if I lived through the disgruntled gym guy ordeal people wouldn't be saying, "You hear about Brent? He told the shooter he *believed in God* just to save his own fuckin' life. Pathetic huh? What a sellout."

Take the Old with the New

[For this post it's helpful to know that I have been reading the Bible and posting updates as I go along. They have quickly become the most popular posts on the blog. The basic idea is that I'm reading the Bible for people that are curious, but don't actually want to read it themselves.]

Regarding my reading and reporting of the Bible someone recently said, "Yeah, but you're reading the Old Testament. Don't most Christians kind of ignore the Old Testament anyway? Don't even they admit that the Old Testament is a bit wacky?"

First of all, I'm reading the Old Testament at the moment because that's the order the book is in.

Second of all, I would say to those people that want to disassociate themselves with Old Testament because it's "a bit wacky", fine, go ahead and disassociate yourself from it. But the fact that many seem to be doing just that suggests to me that they should stop selling the two Testaments together. I mean, if the old one should be disregarded, why include it? And more to the point, you must stop citing the Old Testament altogether then. The 10 Commandments, the Adam and Eve story, Noah's Ark, the miracles, the anti-homosexual stuff, all of it must be now ignored. You can't cherry-pick the parts you like. If you tell me that the bad stuff is just too bad and doesn't apply to modern humans then don't try to convince me of anything else contained in the first half of God's book. If you have judged some parts worthy of being ignored then the entire thing must be as well. Otherwise a fella like me might start suspecting that you are just ignoring the stuff you don't like or agree with, while still trying to advocate the bits that support whatever ideas and opinions you *already have*. You don't get to decide what parts are no longer valid. It's not up to you. I mean, isn't this book the Holy Word of God? Why would he bother writing these things if we're just supposed to now ignore it?

That brings me to point number three. Who are you to decide which parts of God's Word to take to heart and which to ignore anyway? What are the criteria for deciding what is law and what is junk? Are you suggesting God made a mistake by including all that crazy nonsense, such as talking donkeys and the slaughter of thousands of innocent women and children? So God makes mistakes? And *you're* the one to decide what constitutes a Godly mistake and what doesn't?

Fourth of all, is anyone actually trying to claim that there aren't silly or cruel stories in the New Testament?

Thank God for Starving Children!

I just read a poll that said 52% of Americans say that if God does exist they approve of the job he's doing. That's the most fucked up stat I've seen in a long time. So assuming this poll is a scientifically accurate one, these aren't necessarily people that *believe* that God exists; these are people that are saying that *if he does*, he's doing a fine job. *A fine job!* I'm actually at a loss for what to type.

I know there is a chance, and I'm hoping it's the case, that people are just saying that they approve of God's work to sound affable. People do indeed lie to pollsters to make themselves sound better, more proper. So it's quite possible that these people are just saying they approve of God's work to sound positive and optimistic. Or maybe they believe in God and don't wanna badmouth him. We all know how cranky he can be.

But knowing what I do about humans, these folks probably do believe what they said. As sad as that is. All that's wrong with the world, all that I need not mention, and these people think that whoever is controlling it all is doing a *good* job? I don't believe there is someone controlling what happens here on earth. But if I did I'd have to say he was an asshole that didn't give much of a fuck about us. Children with cancer, genocide, rape, famine, *The Bachelor*, nuclear bombs, etc. Why doesn't he step in and give some people a break, the people who deserve it? Surely these people can't believe that a 7-year-old girl being abducted, tortured, raped and killed is A-Okay. That's not a "good job", is it? Surely they would think, *Hey, God....instead of making sure Brenda finds her keys or Frank survives his drunk-driving car crash or little Timmy wins his little league game, why don't you keep those priests away from those kids? Why not make sure no*

145

more babies are born addicted to the drugs their junkie moms were addicted to? Why not—

You know what? I could go on for days about what's wrong and what a loving God could do to pitch in, but what's the point?

<u>This Aggressive Terminal Disease Might Be More Than I Can Handle</u>

Been seeing a lot of those "God will get you through" sayings lately. Of course none of them make a lick of sense if you think about it for half a second. On Facebook yesterday I saw "If God brings you to it, he will bring you through it". And just today I heard a woman on TV say "God doesn't give us more than we can handle."

God doesn't give us more than we can handle?! Do I really need to explain why this saying is so ridiculously stupid? Apply it to a person with cancer. Apply it to a person that has *died* of cancer. Obviously God gave them more than they could handle. Wouldn't you love to see this TV woman say that to a cancer patient on their deathbed? "Come on, Jane. If you couldn't handle this cancer you God wouldn't have given it to you. Suck it up, will ya?"

Brent MacLean

To Kneel or To Act

The Centre for Inquiry Canada created a billboard depicting a smiling woman with some biblical-style phrases, such as "Jenn 13:1, Praying won't help. Doing will." Under the group's name are the words "Without God, We're all Good." The CFIC was told the billboard design was unacceptable.

We actually live in a culture where it's considered "unacceptable" to suggest that _doing_ something is more effective than _hoping_ for something. I find _that_ unacceptable.

I blame passive atheists for the state of things. I do. I'm talking about the people that know better, but choose to remain silent for fear of upsetting religious people. I know a few atheists, total non-believers, that can't stand religion and clearly see the damage it does, that say to religious people, "I don't agree but I totally respect your beliefs." How annoying is that? I've written many times about how beliefs shouldn't automatically garner respect. I would say, "You're free to believe that, but there is **right** and there is **wrong**, there is **fact** and there is **fiction**, and I don't respect any beliefs not based on empirical data." If some Kittichiko Native tells me that man was created when the Great Eagle dropped an egg into a mystical mountain spring which was inhabited by an ancient fish that cared for the egg until it hatched the first human baby who swam to the surface and crawled onto land, I might say that I respect the right to believe it. But there's no way I'm going to say I respect the belief itself. Why? Because it's nonsense and it's based on nothing real. I don't have to call the person stupid or silly, but I definitely don't have to pretend their belief is as valid as any fact.

The constant coddling of believers is bad enough, but it enters Insanity Land when it's considered rude, offensive, and

148

"unacceptable" to suggest that action is better than prayer. You might have noticed that I often refer to praying as hoping, and I do so because that's what it is. Even if you believe prayer works there's no way you believe that it works every time. I've encountered some nutty people but none so nutty as to claim that God answers every single prayer. So even if you're a person that believes in prayer you must admit that since God doesn't answer them all that each individual prayer is essentially asking for a favour. You make a request and hope it gets fulfilled. And that's why I call it hoping. Ask and you or may not receive. And we're seriously telling people that that is better, or at least just as good, as actually doing something? Okay then. Let's start telling our children the same thing. Let's start telling little kids that actually helping someone in need is no better and no more important than hoping (or praying) that the person in need gets the help they require.

Say you have a son. Say he comes home one day and says, "On the way home I saw a little girl lying in a ditch. She was all bloody. I think she was hit by a car. She asked me to help her but I'm gonna go to my room and pray for her instead." What would you tell your son? Unless you're severely mentally deficient you would tell him that he should have actually helped the little girl. You'd ask where the girl is, and you'd tell him that just praying about it is not acceptable. And why would you tell him that? Because you know just as well as I do that prayer is nothing more than hoping for things to get better, and that is as useless as a pig with an abacus. Oh, you can try to tell me that God answers *some* prayers, and I will immediately ask you why he doesn't answer more. I'll ask you why he didn't answer the prayers of the parents that just lost their 2-year-old boy to cancer; or why he didn't answer the prayer of the little girl that just got kidnapped and raped by a neighbour. Then I'll say that since even you admit that God doesn't answer all prayers, you must then admit that action

149

trumps prayer. Because you know only a nutjob would do something as foolish as rely solely on prayer when it comes to something really important; something like, say, a child with a serious illness. Even full-on believers are horrified to hear of parents that choose prayer over medicine. Well, why is that? If you're so confident in the power of prayer, why do you bother with all that silly scientific stuff like medicine and doctors?

If you were honest you would admit that someone praying "I hope he gets home safely" has just as good a chance of getting what they want as I do when I simply say to myself, "I hope he gets home safely." It's chance. It's circumstance. It's odds and likelihood. It's how things play out. Sometimes we get what we want, sometimes we don't. Asking an invisible middleman in the sky to intervene is immature and pointless. And when it comes to one or the other, prayer or action, prayer loses every time. You know it just as well as I do. So again, why would an ad such as the one mentioned above be a problem with anyone? We all know that "doing" will help, but once again we're cowering at the feet of the offended. And *why* are they offended? If they believe that prayer is awesome and that real action isn't any more effective, then fine, that's what *they* believe. What does that have to do with the rest of us? And why are they offended that some rational folks want to say the opposite, that doing is better than praying? How does that affect them and their prayers and their relationship with their God? It doesn't. It's just that they are so used to everyone tiptoeing around them and backing down when they whine about having their opinions challenged. It's time we stop that nonsense. Future generations would be much better off to realize that getting off their knees is the first step to helping other people. But no. The average person would rather the world not improve; that those suffering not get the assistance they desperately need, as long as it means believers don't get their precious feelings hurt. Protecting their egos is evidently more important than effective action.

But I know this about folks that believe in prayer: Their tune would change pretty goddamn quick if they had a child come down with a rare and deadly disease that could be treated if only they had the funds, and people around them said, "No, I'm not gonna donate to your charity, I'm not gonna help you out that way. Instead I'm gonna go home and ask God to just fix it all." I'm quite certain that they would instantly decide that, yeah, *doing is better than praying.*

Toss Another Miracle on the Pile

The people that suddenly find God after they have kids are quite possibly the most annoying people of all. Unless your children survived some kind of accident or serious disease don't refer to them as "miracles". They're not. They're very special to you, I understand, but they're not miracles. An event that appears to be beyond natural laws is a miracle. Being born does not make a person a miracle. Every person was born! Every single person that ever existed was born!

There are over 7,600,000,000 people in the world right now. Seven point six billion. It's a very hard stat to accurately assess, but there is one that estimates that since 50,000BCE there have been 108,000,000,000 people on earth. And that's only in the past 52,000 years. A hundred and eight billion miracles? If something is automatic to every single person that has ever lived, I find it difficult to accept that it can be considered a miracle.

A Very 'Special' God

I think it's time we start classifying the superstitious as mentally challenged. It's either that or call it simple stupidity. Or maybe it's ignorance. Immaturity? Insanity? It's certainly a glitch in mature reasoning. And it's holding our species back. I just read an article about a female runner that pulled out of a race because the bib number she was assigned was 666. How could you not consider this girl at least slightly insane? You can argue for the existence of some intelligent creator of the universe, sure, I'm not surprised some people think that way. But to not only claim you know there is a God, but that you know this God well enough to know that he really cares about what numbers runners wear on their *bibs?* It's just a pretty wacky leap from saying, "I believe the universe was created by some intelligent being" to "This intelligent Creator of the Universe doesn't like that number." Doesn't sound intelligent to me.

"I didn't want to risk my relationship with God and try to take that number," the girl said. Some God you got there, hun, getting all pissed off over a bib number. She really wants us to believe that her God is so unreasonable as to get angry over a number on a bib? This is the shit her God is worrying about? Out of all the horrible and nasty things a human can do, he's concerned with what numbers runners are given? So he gets upset over numbers, but only when they're in a certain sequence. 667 is fine. Even 6766 is fine. But 666 is unacceptable.

Fine then. I'll accept that. But then I think it's time we start to consider God mentally challenged as well.

Brent MacLean

Well, Her Parents Are Religious and I'm Totally Spineless

Christenings. Baptisms. God help me, I just don't get them. What's the deal? Why is it pretty much every religious moderate—and quite a few atheists—go through that silly ceremony? I'm really asking because I do not understand. Every time my wife tells me someone is getting their baby christened I often say, "They're religious?" Of course, the answer is almost always, "They're not. Not really."

"Not really". That's interesting to me because it applies to most of the people I know. They're religious. But they're not. Not really. Just a bit. Just at the edges. Just at the christenings and weddings and funerals. Do these people really think that God is fine with them being "religious, but not really"? According to the Bible he's not. According to the Bible God demands diligence. And if you're saying to yourself, "Well, they don't really believe in God that way," then I have to ask you why in the world then, if they don't really believe in God that way, are they bothering to not only take part in these Christian traditions and ceremonies, but ridicule those that choose not to? It makes no sense at all. Do you believe? Yes? Then follow the rules! And not just two or three times in your whole life! Oh, you don't *really* believe in God? Then why the hell are you pretending you do for these ceremonies, and supporting this religious institution that you don't even believe in?

It's disconcerting that so many atheists still actively partake in these religious rituals and ceremonies. I just don't get these folks. They know it's all nonsense. Many even know it's harmful. But still, they go along. I think of them as the Well-Her-Parents-Are-Religious people, which refers to the answer I most

154

often get when I ask a non-believer why they got married in a church or had their baby baptized: "Well, her parents are religious." (Sometimes it's "my parents" or "his parents" or even "our parents, but you get the idea.) My response to that (that I only say here) is, "Get a backbone. If her parents want to baptize a baby, tell them to have their own baby and to leave yours the hell alone. They want a religious wedding, tell them to get married." It's downright sad how the religious hang-ups of someone's parents can so influence how they run their own lives.

We're not going to baptize our child. A few have asked, "What's your wife's parents think about that?" My stock answer is, "Who cares? It's not their child. They don't have a say." [For the record, they don't seem to care, which tells me they don't truly believe in it in the first place or they'd really be concerned about their granddaughter displeasing God and possibly ending up in hell.] It's hard to respect adults that are afraid of their parents or their spouse's parents. Grow up. Get mature. Think. And do what's right, what's correct, for *you* and *your* children. Let the others run their own lives, not yours.

Whut Up, G?

I love the fact that dead people magically reach into our world all the way from another dimension to communicate with their still-living loved ones via psychics and mediums, and all they say is, "G.... there's a G in my name.... it's a G sound.... *juh, juh....* like that.... a soft G...."

Being an uber-religious person doesn't make you a bad person. Supporting terrible politicians doesn't make you a bad person. Even inconsiderate drivers, as much as they infuriate me, aren't necessarily bad people, even though they act like jerks when behind the wheel. But a person that claims they are psychic, clairvoyant, or a medium *is* a bad person. A terrible person. They take advantage of gullible people; people often in a very vulnerable state, like when grieving over the death of a loved one. They are the lowest of the low.

Would You Know My Username (If I Saw You In Heaven)?

Another awesome Facebook post I just saw:

"I don't know if you can read Facebook in heaven but...."

I know this person is going through some grief at the moment, so I'd like to assure them that yes, Facebook can be read in heaven. It's freakin' *heaven*. You don't think there's gonna be free Wi-Fi?

Brent MacLean

You Must Be This Bipedal to Enter

The 7 most meaningless words in the English language: *My thoughts and prayers are with you.*

I must admit, I find it quite funny that many people are now shortening it to just "Thoughts and prayers". Talk about meaningless! I swear, when something bad happens to me, like the death of a loved one, and I receive the inevitable "thoughts and prayers" comment, there's a strong risk that I might tell them to eat a bag of pigeon dicks. And if someone close to me dies and some prick says, "She's in a better place," I just might ask them to prove it to me, since they seem to be so knowledgeable about what happens after you die. Look, I know people mean well, but it's just a horrible assumption to make. Especially if the person that passed had any kind of family, because you're essentially saying the deceased person would rather be, or are better off, wherever they are now (dead), rather than living with their loved ones. And the same goes for anyone that says I have an angel watching out for me, or that God needed a new angel for his fleet, or something equally moronic. I just might tell them to grow the fuck up and to not talk to me like I'm a child. Why not just tell me my friend didn't really die, that he's just gone to live on a farm?

How am I the only one that's tired of this fluffy stupidity?

I call it fluffy because it's all designed to make people feel warm and fuzzy, regardless of reality or what makes sense. I have no use for such nonsense. Why? Because I have a brain that has this really annoying habit of rationalizing things. That's why I don't believe in angels. Angels. Give me a break, will ya?

I sometimes wonder how many angels there are. When did they start showing up? People seem to think that angels are human only, right? Was heaven empty before that? Did dead people only start showing up at the Pearly Gates when our species showed up (and started dying) 300,000 years ago? Or maybe the other human species that we descended from, and other branches on the tree of human evolution, were post-life heavenly inhabitants. Of course, I suppose it's possible that angels began when apes first started to walk upright. Are there *Australopithecus* angels? *Homo habilis* angels? *Neanderthals* with wings? If so, are they all commingled up there? Because these are different species you know. All of them can't really communicate with one another. Or is it that everyone in heaven automatically speaks the same language, no matter your race or species?

Hey, you folks are the ones that keep talking about angels and heaven. You're the experts. I'm just asking questions.

So imagine heaven, with all these different types of human and bipedal ape species. That's pretty different than the heaven your mama told you about. Angelic cave men and upright apes with massive wings. Awesome, huh? But then again, why would it start at upright apes? Why wouldn't our quadruped ape ancestors get in? Why would they need to be on two feet in order to be admitted? Is that a heavenly requirement? Did I figure it out? "You must be *this* bipedal to enter."

You know how ridiculous this all is. The only difference is I'm honest enough to admit it. Angels and heaven and all that nonsense are just more symptoms of our narcissistic nature. We think we're so special that we get spirit guardians and an eternal afterlife. Let's not even think about the fact that you're actually supposed to be righteous to get into heaven in the first place, because everyone seems believe that they're good enough to get in. You better believe it, boy. If there's one thing people don't lack it's self-righteousness and conceit. She's dead? She's in heaven. He died? Heaven. And I'm so friggin' special that now that poor sap has to watch over *me* for the rest of my life. He's my guardian angel. Hey, let me ask you something. Did you ever think of *asking* Dearly Departed Dave if he even wanted to watch over you? Nah, of course he would. You're just that special. It's not about him anyway. It's about you. It's about us. The living. It's about making us feel better.

Humans. I'm actually embarrassed to be a part of this species. What we say, what we believe; our empty gestures, our pointless traditions; our unwillingness to question anything and our ridicule of those that do. It's depressing and disturbing, this willful ignorance we can't seem to let go of.

I just saw a TV program where a witch was getting a makeover. Yes, a "real" witch. My wife was watching it actually, and I saw the very end. So naturally I was confused. My wife said, "Well, she and her friends live their lives as real witches." I said, "But.... witches aren't real.... these people can't fly... they don't have magical powers... so they essentially are just adults playing dress-up?" The lady went on to say that she was indeed a witch, *and* a psychic. See what I mean? These people should not be allowed to operate. Psychics. Jesus Christ. Yes, adults can play dress-up if they like, that's their choice. But psychics feed upon the gullibility of others, often in great times of distress and grief. It's disgusting and it should be against the law. Until you can prove you have *any* type of psychic abilities you should not be permitted to work as one. (For many years the James Randi Foundation had an open invitation to anyone that wanted to prove they had real psychic abilities. The prize for doing so was a million dollars. It shouldn't surprise you that no one ever demonstrated special powers, so no one ever got the money.)

I made a terrible mistake when I was a child. I trusted adults. Even worse I believed that adults were smarter than children. I believed that they made more sense and had more integrity. I believed that aside from a few bad people, adults didn't lie. For some reason, finding out that adults are more stupid than kids, their lies are worse, and the non-existent ghosts they believe in are far more dangerous, was more of a shock than I ever could have imagined. One that I should be able to get over, but can't. (Why do I say adults are more stupid than children? Because they should know better. Children have an excuse—their brains aren't fully matured. Adults don't have such an excuse.) It wouldn't be so bad if the lies and bullshit were things that adults kept to themselves. But no, they feel the need to pass it on to their kids, and they expect —and often get—special treatment and protection against anything that suggests their lies and bullshit are lies and bullshit. In no intelligent and moral society is that a proper way to operate.

Michael Jackson never got over the fact that he didn't have a childhood. They say that's why he created Neverland. Well, I can't get over the fact that fully grown adults are full of shit. So what should my theme park be called?

<u>You Pray. I'm Confused.</u>

You pray for tumors to go away and diseases to be cured and for surgeries to go well.

You pray for dead loved ones to be happy in some kind of afterlife. You pray for people's pain to subside after tragedy. You pray for money troubles to dissipate. You pray for your child to be successful in life. You pray that you'll find a good parking space. You pray for your team to win the big game. You pray for your concert to go off without a hitch.

But you *don't* pray for lost limbs to regrow. You *don't* pray for loved ones dead and buried to crawl from their graves and live on as if they never died. You *don't* pray for all diseases to disappear forever. You *don't* pray that you attain the ability to fly so you don't have to make the dreadful morning commute anymore. You *don't* pray that the season you hate most no longer occurs. You *don't* pray that every kind of pain ceases to exist. You *don't* pray to go back in time to fix mistakes you made in your past.

Why is that? Why do you never pray for what we know to be impossible? Why do you only pray for things already possible within the laws of physics and nature? Why do you pray only for things that can actually happen without prayer?

<u>Your Old Road</u>

Hopefully this whole anti-gay Arizona law thing has gone as far as it's going to go. Although I'm sure many religious bigots will fight the veto for a while yet. I haven't addressed it but I've been following it. The reason I haven't mentioned it is because it's the 21st Century. We shouldn't even be having these discussions anymore. When it has to do with equality—human equality—I don't think there's much to be said. Either you believe in equality or you don't. I saw a proponent of the law, some Christian woman, on television saying that they are tired of having their beliefs restricted. When the anchor asked her if this bill would allow people to flat-out refuse service to a homosexual she wouldn't say yes or no. She kept answering *around* the question, like Christians often do.

I once had a pastor befriend me online. He seemed nice at first. Turned out he really wasn't at all. Early on I asked him if he was against with gay marriage. He answered, "Doesn't really matter. It's inevitable." See? Another truly Christian answer. In both cases, the lady on television and the pastor, they answered the way they did because the real answer is yes, and they know deep down that the average *decent* person will say that their response is one only an asshole would make. But that's what the potential Arizona law is designed do: Allow people to refuse service to people their God tells them aren't worthy. Otherwise, why even bother with trying to pass the law at all? And by the way, since when has anyone restricted their beliefs? If anything, people have coddled and protected their beliefs. I would only agree with her if she or other Christians were forced to be gay. Then, yes, their beliefs are being restricted. But no one is telling them to become homosexuals, so it's none of their business. Even

163

according to their own claims, their God didn't tell them not to *serve* a homosexual. He told them not to *be* homosexual.

And they can quote the Bible all they want. They can tell me 1000 times that it says in the Bible that homosexuality is an abomination. I know it's in there. But I couldn't care less. The Bible is stupid. And immoral. But as usual, Christians just pick out the rules they like and ignore the ones they don't. Nothing new. But now they expect non-Christians to alter their lives based on those cherry-picked laws?!

What I've found quite disturbing is the support that bill is getting from people that aren't religious; people agreeing with it under the label of the libertarianism. If that's what being a libertarian is then I certainly am not one. I'm probably wrong but I've always thought libertarianism was essentially "do what you wish as long as you don't negatively affect others". But this law would be terribly negative for many people. Imagine, this day and age, three buddies walking down the street. They decide to get some lunch, and one guy says, "Hey, let's go in here; the food's awesome," and one of the friends has to say, "Sorry, man. I'm not allowed to go in there. They won't serve me." That's the world these Christians want to live in! They want to go backwards! Astounding. And disgusting.

I heard one man say, "You should be allowed to refuse service to anyone, no matter what the reason." Ah, no, dingus, you should not. You either serve the public or you don't. What this guy and these people are saying is that they would see nothing wrong with it if businesses started putting "WHITES ONLY" signs up in their windows again. How is it any different? They are essentially saying "HETEROSEXUALS ONLY". You want to stop black people, or gay people, or redheads from going into your house? Fine. It's your house. Stop whomever your hateful little heart desires. But when you open a store or business to the public you no longer get to decide what type of person is allowed to use it. You operate a commercial business which means you are inviting the public into your establishment; not select members.

I'm assured again and again that despite these things, the United States is heading in the right direction; that racism, homophobia, religious nutbaggery are all on the decline. It probably is, although I'm not convinced. They certainly do seem to have an inordinate amount of people still getting their twisted morals from Bronze Age myths, and that is precisely why it's so important to denounce religion and no longer give it the protection it has enjoyed for all these years. It's up to the people that know better to stop this nonsense.

The lyrics to Bob Dylan's anthemic *The Times They Are a-Changin'* were written for people just like these primitive Arizonians. The waters have grown around their little world and flooded their little minds, and they're in a panic; they feel they're drowning. They despise progress. And it has nothing to do with God—don't let them fool you. They're just using religion as a shield, as justification to act upon their repulsive opinions. If it really was about the Bible and God they would never eat shellfish or work on Sundays. They're picking the rule that supports the hate they already possess.

Brent MacLean

Keep Calm and Defend Reason

"The world is a dangerous place; not because of those who do evil, but because of those who look on and do nothing"
- Albert Einstein

I've mentioned many times that I think the people that deserve the most criticism when it comes to the issue of reason and education are not the religious, but the religious moderates, and even more so, the passive atheists. It's the fence-sitters; those non-believers that tell the superstitious, "I don't agree with your beliefs but I respect them."; the "I'm an atheist too but I don't need to talk about it" people; the "spreading atheism is the same as spreading religion" people; the people that protect the beliefs and institutions of religious terrorists; the people that know the difference; the people that know there were never talking snakes but still pretend it's a rational and sensible thing for an adult to believe. I recently said to an atheist friend, "It's really the fault of atheists, the rational, that the world is still so full of shit. We have the power to change things. We know better. But most people not only ignore it all, they encourage it." The friend said, "So you want me to risk my friendship and my work relationships to tell people they are full of shit?"

Now, this always irritates me. I've said many times that I expect no one to go around tearing down people and their beliefs. I expect no one to go full-on militant atheist whenever someone says "God bless you." Pick your spots; don't risk relationships unless your integrity is at stake, which is a situation you will rarely, if ever, find yourself in. I'm saying don't pretend you're a believer just because people around you are. Don't be afraid to say, "I don't believe that." Don't be apologetic for not being a believer.

Don't say, "I'm sorry, I just don't believe." That sounds like you're saying there's something wrong about being a non-believer. Don't be afraid to say that your beliefs are based in fact only. Don't be afraid to say you believe children should be allowed to grow up and decide for themselves which, if any, religion makes the most sense to them. Don't call people stupid and try not to laugh if someone brings up something ridiculous (like the Adam and Eve story for instance). If you remain jovial most often the believers will too. There will always be hardcore nutcases though, but most people aren't. Don't take yourself too seriously, yet don't compromise your sense of reason. "I just don't see any evidence" is a near perfect sentence because it really sums it all up. If you sense someone getting angry or you see the conversation is becoming a much-too-long discussion, just clue it up. If you get one believer to think—actually think—about what it really is they're going along with, I would call that a great win.

It's about questions. It's about facts and education. It's about no longer blindly following something because your mommy told you to. But more than that it's about you staying strong in the assertion that reason and evidence trumps superstition every time. You're not going to throwaway logic to please others. That's the most important thing. Logic spent centuries suppressed by religious belief but those days should be over. And one way to help that along is to not shy away from conversations with believers. One thing I've noticed, and I'd be curious to know if any of you have experienced the same thing, is that almost every discussion I've ever had with a believer eventually ends up with the person saying, "Well, I mean, I don't know. Nobody really knows." I love that moment. I get to say, "That's what I'm saying." That tells me they are atheist and they don't even know it. Unless you answer with an unequivocal "Yes" when asked "Do you believe in God?" then you are atheist. You are atheist because the answer is not yes. If I ask you, "Do you believe your house exists?" you would say yes without any doubt or hesitation. You believe your house is really there; it exists. But if you can't say the same about God then you're atheist, my friend. You're *a-theist*; you are *not a theist*.

Things may very well be more complicated in your family or circle of friends to apply anything I've said here. Maybe you have some angry religious people that get really upset whenever anyone even questions God's existence. Those people exist. I know of a few around me but I haven't had the pleasure of discussing religion with them. On more than one occasion I've heard from some third party, "Oh, don't say that around _____, he/she'll get really upset." One thing I've noticed is that none of the super-sensitive people that have gotten mad at me are churchgoers. And not one of them has read the Bible. None of them were what one might call a religious fanatic. That's not that surprising to me though. For one, most believers aren't church-going Bible readers. Also, if they had actually read the Bible they deem so important, there's less likely a chance they'd believe in it. (I know, believing in a book you haven't read is an odd idea. But millions do just that.) I hope I'm not contradicting myself here. I also hope it's not coming off like I'm trying to tell anyone what to do. I'm not. I'm simply saying what I would like to see people do; what I think needs to happen to move this species along the intellectual evolutionary line; what I think needs to be done to rid the world of harmful superstitious nonsense. And no, like I said, I don't think you have to risk your family cutting you out of their lives just so you can stand up for yourself. I must say, I think that's a horrific thing for someone to do, to shun a friend or family member solely because of their beliefs or lack thereof.

But I certainly know it's done all the time. Strangers have contacted me online and told me they have been shunned by their family members because they announced they were atheist. Speaking for myself, I know my family (I'm talking about immediate family) would never cut me off for that reason. They're all atheists anyway, even if a couple of them are reluctant to admit it. But when it comes to relatives outside my immediate family? Couldn't care less. If someone wants to talk about it I will, and if they end up getting super angry and all that because I don't respect groundless beliefs, then so be it. It doesn't bother me one iota if someone wants nothing to do with me because I don't believe in talking snakes and zombie carpenters. If someone cuts you off for such a thing, that's their problem, not yours. I hate religion, absolutely, but I have never shunned another person because of their beliefs. Ever. I just wouldn't do such a thing. "Believe what I believe or I want nothing to do with you." If a person is wacky enough to say that to me then I'm probably better off without them. Obviously they are dangerously intolerant.

I guess I should try to sum up my point. Just don't ever be embarrassed or afraid to be a person that doesn't blindly follow some religious dogma. That's a reason to be proud, not shy. You wouldn't want your child to believe without question all the tall tales he heard at school. You'd want him to think critically. That's a major part of maturing and intelligence. We should all be critical thinkers. Don't go along with the idea that being religious somehow makes a person 'more moral', because I know you how ridiculous an idea that is.

And another thing. If you do have the occasional conversation about God, don't let people convince you that that topic is off limits. No topic is off limits if two people want to discuss it.

Now I Lay Me Down to Die

If my child asks me if there are any ghosts in this house I will explain to her that they do not exist. If she's old enough to understand a little bit of reasoning I will tell her the reasons that I know they don't exist. If she's too young then I'll hope she trusts me enough to take me at my word. If she asks if there really is a Bigfoot roaming the countryside I will tell her it's not true. If she asks if people really get abducted by aliens I will tell her that it doesn't happen and the people that claim they were abducted are either starving for attention or mentally ill.

But what do I tell her when she asks why people go to a building with a pointy roof to ask an invisible man in the sky for special favours?

I have no idea how this child raising thing will play out. But I can guarantee you she will not be going to bed at night chanting things like:

Now I lay me down to sleep
I pray the Lord my soul to keep
If I should die before I wake
I pray the Lord my soul to take

She will not lie in her bed thinking and worrying about dying in her sleep, hoping that God will answer her prayer to take her soul to heaven, instead of letting the devil drag her to hell. She will not lie in bed wondering if she followed the 10 Commandments well enough that day to please God. She will not lie there thinking that the ghosts of her dead relatives are roaming around her house, just outside her bedroom. She will not wonder why a God that says he loves her would allow her to burn for an eternity if she doesn't follow his strange rules. She will not wonder what's going to happen to the souls of the millions and millions of people that were unlucky enough to have been born in a place where the wrong religion was prevalent, thus making it near impossible that they should believe in the correct God and find true happiness.

The religious hatred, the physical and mental abuse, the oppression of women, the violence and hatred toward homosexuals, the childhood indoctrination and abuse, and the suppression of science—all these things persist not because of the religious. It's because of the *non*-religious people. It's the one-church-visit-per-year folks. It's the "I believe in the Bible even though I haven't read it" people. It's the people that are only religious on Facebook. It's the people that pretend to be religious on their wedding day; or when a friend dies; or when a baby gets its name. It's silent atheists. It's people that are afraid to confront the irrationality and hypocrisy of religion that are ensuring that these superstitions and all the terrible things that stem from them continue unabated, because they choose to tip-toe around the believers, deathly afraid of offending them by suggesting that their unfounded beliefs are unfounded. They hold the power to change things for the better but knowingly—*purposefully*—choose not to. And that's a terrible thing. It's an *immoral* thing.

Well, I choose to. I choose to try to change things for the better. People say to me, to people like me, "You're not going to change the world." No, I will not change the world. But I've received enough messages from people that have struggled with religious upbringings to know I'm doing a good thing, and that I am, even if it's only in some minuscule way, helping them deal with their complicated situations. And what about the people that know that it's all a sham but aren't great at thinking the whole thing through cohesively and coherently? What if a few posts from me or someone like me snaps everything into place for them, making them more resolved, more certain in what they already know deep down? I had one fellow tell me that my blogging helped him to argue against the angry religious people that populated the town in which he worked. He was already an atheist, but he just wasn't great at explaining things. This guy even told me that a person that he once argued with came back to him later and said, "Man, I've been thinking a lot about what you said, and I gotta say, you're right." You're right! He changed a person's mind! And he says I helped!

So no, I'm not changing the world. But who says that should be your only goal? Who says it has to be all or nothing? Do you say that to someone that works for a charity? Do you tell people that trying to help starving children on the other side of the world is pointless because your donation will not eradicate starvation? Do you tell people, "Nah, I'm gonna keep my $5 because I'm sure cancer won't be completely and totally cured if I give it to your charity"? Of course you don't. Because you know these things are *processes*.

Change takes time. Progress takes time. Often these things take efforts from multitudes of people; people chipping away at whatever problem they wish to change. I'm sure there were people that said to the folks trying to eradicate slavery, "Come on. It's the way it is! It's been like that forever! It's tradition! You think that you and a few others big-mouths yapping about it is going to change anything?"

Slavery didn't end because of one single person. It was a tragically brutal road to emancipation traveled by millions of people, but the goal was reached, eventually. Sure, the people at the beginning of that or any other struggle might not have lived to see the offending disease, virus, or cruelty disappear or get corrected. But does that mean they wasted their time? They got the ball rolling. They opened people's eyes, even if it was only on a person-by-person basis. Any major change in a society is never accomplished by one soul. It's always a vast movement of changing ideas and perception over a given period of time. Think of it as a chain of change. And that period of change may be stretched over years, it may be decades, it may be millennia. It doesn't matter to the people that get to enjoy the changes set in motion by past problem solvers they will never meet.

The Greek proverb "A society grows great when old men plant trees whose shade they know they shall never sit in" is precisely what I'm getting at. I'm an old man planting a tree (along with hundreds of thousands of other people planting trees). Let's call it a tree of knowledge, because that's the intent: to spread knowledge; to encourage education, objectivity, and critical thought; to let people know that we're not all going to bend like weaklings under the force of superstition and religion that has weighed down humanity since our thoughts became abstract. For the first time we have the ability to control our own evolution. This is evolution of the mind. We can make changes in our thinking today that will benefit the world tomorrow.

No, I will not live to see any worldly benefit from what I or people like me have said over the past few years. I won't sit under that tree of knowledge because there are still too many shrubs of delusions stealing the light and enjoying protection from rational thought. I won't sit under the tree but I have seen the roots getting deeper. I've seen the tiny sprouts breaking through the dirt. I've seen them in the messages I've received from people, thanking me and encouraging me to keep doing what I'm doing.

But all that aside, I'm absolutely sure of one thing. I have the power to change my daughters' world, and I will not let people fill her head with all the delusions that filled mine as a child. And I will not fill her head with superstitions and fairy tales designed to scare her into believing in things that any rational person, any loving parent, would and should wholeheartedly protect their children from. I might even teach her a different rhyme:

173

Brent MacLean

Now I lay me down to sleep
My dreams will be my own to keep
In the morning I will awake
Learn something new with each step I take

CPSIA information can be obtained
at www.ICGtesting.com
Printed in the USA
LVHW092325030120
642538LV00001B/51/P

9 780359 664719